THE BIBLE AND LITURGY

The Bible and Liturgy

E. H. van Olst

Translated by John Vriend

WILLIAM B. EERDMANS PUBLISHING COMPANY
GRAND RAPIDS, MICHIGAN

Library of Congress Cataloging-in-Publication Data

Olst, E. H. van (Evert H.)
   [Bijbel en liturgie. English]
   The Bible and liturgy / E. H. van Olst; translated by John Vriend.
     p.   cm.
   Translation of: Bijbel en liturgie.
   ISBN 0-8028-0306-7 (pbk.)
   1. Liturgics. 2. Bible — Liturgical use. 3. Reformed Church —
Liturgy. I. Title.
BV176.045 1991
264 — dc20   91-13550
                                         CIP

Contents

Acknowledgments

Several people were delightfully willing to help me reproduce in English some of the Dutch poems and songs that are interspersed in the text. Among them I wish to single out for special thanks Dr. Martin Bakker, Professor of Germanic Languages at Calvin College; Dr. Henry Baron, Professor of English at Calvin College; and Dr. Howard Slenk, Professor of Music at Calvin College. In addition, I owe a debt of gratitude to Rabbi Michael Rascoe and his wife Marcy, both of Ahavas Israel in Grand Rapids, Michigan, for explaining to me parts of the synagogue liturgy and welcoming me to their celebration of Simchat Torah.

John Vriend

Introduction

In many churches today there is a growing interest in the practice of worship. Whereas in the Roman Catholic tradition the liturgy was always a central field of concern, in most mainline Protestant communions in North America what happens in a worship service has only recently been rediscovered.

In Roman Catholic circles, however, there has also been a ferment of rediscovery, with much happening there as a result of reflection on biblical backgrounds, the introduction of vernacular language, and a greater emphasis on congregational participation in worship.

Here one can even speak of mutual benefits. The explanation of Scripture in Catholic worship has become much more significant, whereas among Protestants the classic Roman missal has been discovered as a source of biblical-liturgical relationships.

A wealth of liturgical literature has been showered on the member churches of various denominations, much of it showing the influence of classical patterns of worship. The publication of new songbooks especially serves to stimulate interest in liturgy. Pilot projects — places of liturgical incubation where new ideas could be tested and tried — have not been lacking.[1]

1. See, for example, P. Oskam, *Liturgische broedplaatsen* (Kampen: Kok, 1973).

Manifest in all of this has been a deepening awareness on the part of church members of their place and task in church and society, an awareness that has led naturally to the raising of questions concerning the order and organization of the worship services.

However, all these hopeful signs notwithstanding, in any number of churches the liturgy is still given short shrift. In these circles one often hears it said that what counts, after all, is the sermon; the rest is secondary. Upon further inquiry one discovers that preaching and proclamation are mistakenly equated, though proclamation is clearly a much larger category. Thus, for example, in the prayers and songs that accompany the Scripture readings — when they are carefully chosen and wisely used — there are clear components of proclamation.

Furthermore, proclamation is but one focus in the service; at the very least, adoration and praise constitute a second. However, in Protestant circles this latter dimension has hardly been realized. For numerous churchgoers the most important reason for going to church is to hear a sermon, the remaining parts of the service being generally regarded as its introduction or appendage.

In general, people do not know why certain things take place in a worship service. When some of them begin to realize that more is going on than the tradition of the "one-man show" suggests — that in fact people come together to celebrate the mighty acts of God and that they want to be personally and actively involved in them, that "the shape of the liturgy" is an essential issue — then a multitude of problems rise to meet them. Some sense intuitively that things must change, but those who feel that way often cannot articulate their feelings very well, and they frequently experience little understanding from others. The resulting impasse is hard to get beyond.

The standard objections are well known. "What counts," the objectors say, "is the proclamation of the message of salvation; the rest is frills." "Liturgy is Catholic," or "liturgy is high-church fuss and bother." Calvin too is said to have had little use for it.

Introduction

Many have the idea that by and large things have always
been done the way they are done now, apart from certain periods of decline like the Middle Ages when the "papal mass
held sway." As a rule churchgoers are amazed to discover that,
liturgically speaking, churches of the Calvinist sort occupy a
rather strange and exceptional position in the world church. If
on top of this they also come to realize that this exceptional
position is due, in large measure, to the "spirit of the times" in
which it took shape, to the intellectualism that came up like a
flood after the Renaissance, then it really is time for them to
take another look.

At this point one soon discovers that even an appeal to
Calvin to justify the weakened practice that has developed, in
many instances fails to make sense. To be sure, Calvin had no
room in the worship service for musical instruments, but he
did powerfully stimulate congregational singing. Not only
were the Psalms put to verse, but also the canticles of the New
Testament and parts of the daily services were given a place.
Hymn singing — something on which Calvin's successors
failed to follow through — was part of this program of renewal.
For that reason an appeal to Calvin in support of singing only
Psalms in the worship services is bound to fail.[2]

Further, from time to time people seek to legitimate the
free choice of texts as opposed to following a lectionary by
saying that Calvin abolished the classic order of the church
year. They tend to forget, however, that Calvin advocated the
practice of *lectio continua* (the systematic public reading from
Sunday to Sunday of the books of the Bible), so that the church
would not be subjected to the momentary whims of the
preacher. Another fallacy is that to follow a certain established
order would violate the freedom of the Word. Freedom should
not be confused with individualism. It may be a common thing
to do but it remains false. True freedom does not harm the
church. However, the kind of individualistic notion just referred to does render a disservice to the church.

2. L. Brink, *De eredienst* (Den Haag: Boekencentrum, 1979), p. 80.

By this sort of individualism we keep the other members of the church uninvolved and voiceless. What could be more normal than the opportunity to prepare oneself for important events, in this case the Sunday worship service? Having said that, we have not yet breathed a word about the organist or the church choir, or about the integration of the proclamation of the Word with other activities in the church.

The position that an ordered structure, specifically the use of a lectionary, implies a restriction is not justified. Since in no situation can one avoid making a choice, what counts is making a responsible choice. Furthermore, the practice of permitting a free choice of text generally leads to a much narrower range of themes.

But having said all this, we have not yet touched upon the essence of a liturgical event. Why liturgy? Why celebrate? This is the sort of question with which one is soon confronted when addressing the issue of "the shape of the liturgy." The question "why?" is important for two reasons.

In the first place, the answer to this question has priority over any more detailed address to liturgical formation. Only after the "why?" has been answered can the question "how?" be resolved. In the second place, it is necessary to give an account to all those involved of what one does in liturgy, not only to be able to give a satisfactory answer to curious questioners but especially to raise the consciousness of people concerning the reasons why one does things; for, as the Jewish saying goes: "Forgetfulness leads to exile but remembering is the secret of redemption" (Baal Shem-Tov).

The central thesis of this book is that the structure of celebration is a given that comes with Scripture itself. In terms of both origin and use the Bible can be called a liturgical book. This fact is self-evident when it comes to the five books of the Psalms. It is less well known that, apart from the Psalms, some seventy additional songs occur in Scripture, among which are the familiar canticles of Miriam, Hezekiah, Simeon, Zechariah, and others. In addition, many stories have a liturgical "setting," such as the story of the Exodus, the story of the entry into

Canaan (Joshua), and the many liturgical moments (and fragments) in the book of Revelation.

The Bible can also be called a liturgical book in view of the
manner in which it functioned (and often still functions). The
main currents in the history of this functioning of Scripture will
be briefly examined in this volume. It concerns the Jewish tradition, the early Christian tradition as it eventually took shape in
the classic church year, and the Calvinistic tradition. This latter
tradition will be viewed particularly in the light of modern
thought (beginning with the Renaissance). Not enough attention
has been paid to the fact that the liturgical decline evident in this
tradition is related to the rise of subjectivism and individualism
and the continuing undervaluation of human corporeality.

The acknowledgment of these latter influences will lead
us back to the truth that foundational to our involvement with
Scripture as a liturgical book are certain underlying anthropological (and psychological) notions. The world of the Bible
presupposes the existence of a certain structure of experience
in the person who celebrates. The nature and fortunes of this
structure will be discussed.

Our contact with the Bible takes place not primarily by
way of concepts but by way of images. The language of the
Bible is mainly metaphorical and symbolic, poetic and mythical. This fact leads us to the imagination as a "knowing" function, to the nature of poetic experience, and to the "mythical"
mind. We shall also consider the ordering of human existence
in time — the relationship between nature and history — as
well as the corporeality of human beings. In worship, according
to the biblical perspective, not just the human mind but the
whole of human existence, including human corporeality, is
involved. According to biblical criteria it is the purpose of
human beings to praise God with their entire existence. We
shall find that from this point of view the split between thought
and action will disappear, that experience and expression
belong together, that worship and ethics as faith-governed
human action presuppose rather than oppose each other. For
worship this means the restoration of the language of the body

as it comes to expression in sound and movement. But what is our present situation? Just what are the possibilities for renewal? What road can the churches take? How can the intellectualism prevailing in the liturgy be overcome?

This book is intended primarily for people interested in what happens in a worship service and who perhaps participate in liturgical work groups. But a number of the viewpoints discussed here are significant for others too. This book is intended to be both popular and scholarly. Footnotes will be kept to a minimum and considerations of a theoretical and terminological nature will be avoided as much as possible.

Little attention will be devoted to the more material aspects of the liturgy, other than what is needed to illustrate the points made. Excellent books on these aspects already exist.

The focus of this little book will be the question of which anthropological notions are involved, from within a biblical viewpoint, in a liturgical celebration. Another way of saying this is, What is the nature and structure of the experience of celebrating humans? The world of human experience is not a fixed entity but a mirror of cultural change. As far as Western culture is concerned we can say that in preceding centuries the world of human experience has become considerably smaller in more than one respect, a contraction that makes contact with the biblical world of life and thought more difficult. In this respect a renewed acquaintance with the world of the Bible can be broadening as well as enriching. For that reason the issue of liturgical celebration has importance for those outside the church as well.

1. *The Liturgical Structure of the Bible*

The liturgical practice of Israel and the early church played a large role in the formation and final redaction of the Bible. The extent of that influence is evident, among other things, from the fact that when the church formed the canon the liturgical use of a given Bible book was one of the most important criteria. In this chapter we shall discuss several aspects of the liturgical structure of the Bible. First, we shall reflect on the liturgical origin of many parts of the Bible and on the influence of a liturgical point of view on the composition of larger units such as Bible books.

We shall then ask how in this connection the relationship between the Old and the New Testament should be viewed and what the nature of the unity of the Bible is. We shall focus on *remembering* as the central concern of our interaction with the Scriptures. We shall also take a look at the language of the Bible — a language of imagery — as well as at the biblical symbols. In conclusion, we shall discuss the sabbath and the church festivals as times when remembering is central.

1. The Liturgical Origin

The most striking example of this kind of book, of course, is the Psalms, the songbook, but particularly the prayer book, of

Israel and the church. It is characteristic of the Psalms that in them prayer and praise constitute a unity. (Using the Psalms as Scripture readings does violence to their character!)

As C. Westermann has pointed out, in the Psalms one discovers two poles, lament and praise, which manifest themselves in psalms of lament and psalms of praise.[1] Our humanity moves between these two poles, poles that come together in petition and thanksgiving and in this form may constitute *one* prayer.

The Psalms had a place in the liturgy of the temple. During and after the Exile — a period in which the synagogue developed, not so much to replace the ministry of the temple as to deepen the spiritual life of the people[2] — the Psalms begin to form an integral part of synagogal worship. One can even say that the liturgy of the synagogue originated, in large part, from the Psalms. Praise, however, was not restricted to the services of worship. Praise was an integral part of the existence of the Old Testament believers, for God is "enthroned on the praises of Israel" (Ps. 22:3). Praise is at the heart of human existence: the dead cannot praise God (Ps. 6:5). One does not have to look hard to find this theme also in the other books of the Old Testament (for example, in Job 1:21; Isa. 38:18).

It is a feature of the Psalms that not only human beings are summoned to praise; all creatures are. "Praise the LORD from the earth, you sea monsters and all deeps" (Ps. 148:7-13). Thus praise is much broader than the cultic song that only human beings can sing. Besides the praise that arises from the whole of creation there is also the lament, because "we know that the whole creation has been groaning in travail" (Rom. 8:22). We may conclude therefore that within the liturgical framework of the Psalms the whole of the created world functions in praise and finds the meaning of its existence there. This is a broader perspective than people generally have.

1. Claus Westermann, *Praise and Lament in the Psalms* (Atlanta: John Knox, 1981).

2. Shmuel Safrai, *Das Jüdische Volk im Zeitalter des Zweiten Tempels* (Neukirchen-Vluyn: Neukirchener Verlag, 1978), chap. 9.

However, the Psalms are not the only liturgical songs in the Bible. It also contains songs other than psalms called canticles. Well-known canticles include the song of Moses (Ex. 15), the song of Deborah (Judg. 5), the song of Hannah (1 Sam. 2), and, in the New Testament, the songs of Zechariah, Mary, and Simeon. In the synagogue all readings from the Torah and the prophets were (and are) sung (recited) by the cantor, as well as the so-called festive scrolls, that is, Song of Solomon, Ruth, Lamentations, Ecclesiastes, and Esther. It is not clear in all cases how far the roots of this practice reach back into biblical times. In addition to the sung portions of Scripture (called cantillations), there are prayer chants that go back to temple days.[3]

In the ancient church one may observe an increasing use of the canticles.[4] Origen mentions them and Athanasius recommends that in the morning prayer the so-called *Benedicite Dominum* (also known as the *Canticle of the Three Youths in the Fiery Furnace*, Dan. 3:52-90, JB) be sung. This has been called one of the greatest hymns of synagogue and church. According to Rufinus (ca. 400), this canticle was sung throughout the church.

Another canticle we have already mentioned, the song of Moses and Miriam (Ex. 15), was sung in the ancient church at baptism during the Easter Vigil. The song of Moses (Deut. 32), the song of the strong city (Isa. 26), the prayer of Jonah (Jon. 2), and Hezekiah's song of thanksgiving (Isa. 38) also deserve mention here. Initially the use of the canticles seems to have been more extensive in the East, but after some time they proved to be in vogue also in the West.

In addition to Exodus 15 and Deuteronomy 32, the ancient liturgies included the prayer of Habakkuk (Hab. 3) on Good Friday and the song of the vineyard (Isa. 5) in the Easter Vigil. We may conclude that the Old Testament canticles also functioned this way in the early church and later.

3. Abraham Millgram, *Jewish Worship* (Philadelphia: Jewish Publication Society of America, 1971), pp. 365-366.
4. See "Biblical Canticles" in the *New Catholic Encyclopedia*, vol. 3 (New York: McGraw-Hill, 1967), pp. 69-70.

Canticles occur not only in the Old Testament but also in the New. In addition to those already mentioned, several others come to mind. "Awake, O sleeper, and arise from the dead, and Christ shall give you light" (Eph. 5:14) gets a place in the Easter Vigil. From the book of Revelation we learn that in matters of liturgy the early Christians very closely followed the Torah and the prophets. For example, in the song of the four living creatures (Rev. 4:8b) we find "Holy, holy, holy, is the Lord God Almighty," a reference to Isaiah 6:3, where the trisagion ends with "the whole earth is full of his glory." The Isaiah passage has been incorporated into all the classic eucharistic liturgies as the so-called Sanctus. Praise, we saw in the Old Testament, is the central component in human existence. The same motif marks the entire book of Revelation. It is a liturgical book through and through, steeped in Old Testament words and images. Its liturgical function appears clearly from the introduction (1:4-8), where we encounter an elaborate greeting, blessing, and doxology.[5] The church is described as a kingdom of priests, of liturgists, a reference to Exodus 19:6: "And you shall be to me a kingdom of priests."

Liturgy, as Cromphout remarks in his book on the Apocalypse, is "to confess and to sing, in the presence of God, that there is salvation; and to say that he alone is the Ruler over all things, and thus to break the enchantment of the world and its power."[6] This liturgical setting at the same time constitutes the practical relevance of Revelation. Within this framework the interpretation of one's own time takes place; it did in the first century and it does now, for the same powers and forces are still at work. The book is full of liturgical directions. It had its beginning on a Sunday. "I was in the Spirit on the Lord's day" (1:10). From this book especially it becomes clear that the language of the Bible is not the language of objective information,

5. For the Jewish liturgical backgrounds, cf. Pierre Prigent, *Apocalypse et liturgie* (Neuchâtel, 1964).
6. F. Cromphout, *Hoelang nog een pad door de Apokalyps* (Leuven: Acco, 1979), p. 16.

but the visionary, poetic language of seers, dreamers, and poets, the language of symbols, liturgy, and witness.

Chapter 5 depicts a grand liturgical event. The four living creatures and the twenty-four elders sing a new song (v. 9) followed by a great doxology to the Lamb — hymns that are charged with great political relevance, for the power of the emperor is expressly transferred to the Lamb. In this as well as in the previous chapter we witness how the liturgy is celebrated in heaven — by angels, the twenty-four elders, the saints, the four living creatures — in short, by the entire creation (the four living creatures represent the cosmos). The church on earth, together with and on behalf of the whole creation, takes part in that liturgy, "for the creation waits with eager longing for the revealing of the sons of God" (Rom. 8:19). Also, the song of the conquerors in chapter 15, called the song of Moses and the song of the Lamb (v. 3), has its origin in the Old Testament. (For this, see Jer. 10:6, 7a and Ps. 86:9.) The cry of hallelujah, familiar to us from the Psalms and the synagogal liturgy, occurs repeatedly in chapter 19. The marriage supper of the Lamb, which served as model for the eucharistic meals of early Christians, is also mentioned in this chapter. These few examples suffice to show that Revelation is particularly rich in liturgical material that functioned, one way or another, in the early Christian churches.

But in the remaining books of the New Testament one also finds liturgical fragments — such as prayers in Acts 4:24ff., of course the Lord's Prayer, as well as confessional statements like Philippians 2:6-11. In addition, there are hymns, doxologies, and liturgical formulas.

There is reason to think that many parts of the Old and the New Testament were used in Jewish and/or ancient Christian liturgies.[7] Scholars have suggested that a large part of the book of Exodus was written as a Jewish Passover liturgy.[8] In

7. W. F. Golterman, *Liturgiek* (Haarlem: Bohn, 1951), chap. 6.
8. M. A. Beek, *A Journey Through the Old Testament* (London: Hodder and Stoughton, 1959), p. 64.

any case, the Exodus story clearly consists of information about a sacrificial feast that occurs in the spring of the year, about a spring festival of unleavened barley bread, and about the practice of sacrificing the firstborn of the flock and the firstfruits of the harvest.[9] All this material has been woven into the one story of the Exodus. There are probably a number of concrete historical "cores" in the story but the focus is prophetic: it is told with a view to "remembering"; it serves a liturgical structure. Within this framework the historicizing of the spring festivals took place. A very clear instance of this occurs in the song of Moses, where Israel is described as passing through a petrified sea of nations (Ex. 15:16) which takes the place, as it were, of the passage through the Sea of Reeds. The purpose of the story, therefore, is not so much to reproduce what we call the historical facts as to depict "the pathway which is threatened, but which is made safe by Yahweh and so leads to its goal."[10] At issue here is the basic structure of the saving acts of God, which also can be found in the story of his leading Israel into the land of Canaan. It is in this structure that the remembrance of Israel as well as the liturgical celebration of the church is rooted.

We have now come to the second point: the influence of the liturgical viewpoint on the composition of the whole. We shall first illustrate this perspective by referring to the book of Joshua as a completed unit. Next we shall examine the relationship between the composition of the canon and its liturgical functioning.

The story of the entry into Canaan as recorded in Joshua reveals a liturgical setting.[11] The fact that what Joshua offers is not historical reportage is already evident from the circumstance that in the Hebrew canon Joshua is numbered among the prophets. Since in the canon as the church operates with it Joshua is counted among the historical books, we must pause

9. N. A. van Uchelen: *Exodus 1-20* (Kampen: Kok, 1980), chap. 5.
10. N. Lohfink, *The Christian Meaning of the Old Testament* (Milwaukee: Bruce Publishing, 1968), p. 84.
11. K. A. Deurloo, *Jozua: Verklaring van een bijbelgedeelte* (Kampen: Kok, 1981).

a moment to ask why in the Hebrew canon it is the first of the prophetic books.

The original composition, known as the Palestinian or Hebrew canon and currently described as the Tanak, is concentric in nature. One can speak of concentric fields "situated" around the core, which is the Torah of Moses. The prophets (*Nebiim*) are "situated" around this core and form the second concentric field. The writings (*Kethubim*) form the third such concentric field. The whole, deriving its name from the initials of the three main groups, is called Tanak. But when in the third century B.C. the Tanak was translated into Greek (the so-called Septuagint) for the benefit of Diaspora Jews who could no longer read the Hebrew, the order of the books was changed. Also, the Septuagint contained more books than the Tanak.

The concentric structure of the Tanak then made way for a quasi-historical one. The Torah and what the Tanak called the Former Prophets (Joshua, Judges, I and II Samuel, I and II Kings), together with a number of other books (Ruth, I and II Chronicles, Ezra, Nehemiah, and Esther), are now described as the historical books. What the Tanak called the Latter Prophets (Isaiah through Malachi) in the Septuagint became the prophets. The remainder was placed in the class of poetic books. While the church adopted the Septuagint as canon, the Jews put it aside around the beginning of the Christian era and went back to the original structure of the Tanak. The churches of the Reformation returned to the Tanak, but the order remained that of the Septuagint. This had radical consequences for the interpretation and liturgical use of the Bible. For Joshua became a historical book instead of a prophetic history oriented to the future. The resulting problems are nicely illustrated by the archeological fact that at the time of the entry Jericho and Ai had been heaps of ruins for some centuries.

In the New Testament, as is evident from Luke 24:44, the order of the Tanak is presupposed. Hence we are in good company when we regard Joshua as a prophetic book. We have already referred to the liturgical setting of this book. On the occasion of the entry (Josh. 5) the Passover is celebrated with the

Promised Land in full view. This story was put in writing after the debacle of the captivity, that is, after the ultimate failure of the entry. Thus Joshua shows that the true entry into the Promised Land still has to take place. There is here really no conquest story. (By this time Jericho and Ai were no longer existing cities.) It is not a historical report but a prophetic dream. W. Barnard refers to the fact that at some point during the Exile the word for "conquer" was apparently given a different meaning.[12] At least in the Septuagint it is repeatedly translated by "inherit" or "to receive in trust." (Later Jesus uses the same word when he says that the meek will inherit the earth.)

The prophecy of Joshua received its shape in the liturgical events recorded in the book. The entry, like the Exodus, was marked by liturgical celebration. The land that is described is improbably large — from Egypt to the Euphrates. Even under David the kingdom never attained that size. But one must listen to the story with the ears of "the person in bondage who, instructed by God, prepares himself to enter the broad land of liberty." "With a few surrealistic strokes it is realistically put on the map, for that land is *here*."[13] Already within the Israelite context it is a liturgical context. The character of a celebration or commemoration is clearly shown in the story of the passage through the Jordan (Josh. 3, 4). At the end of three days, after the people had arrived at the Jordan, in procession behind the ark of the covenant and the priests, they crossed the Jordan. Twelve memorial stones were set up. "When your children ask in time to come, 'What do those stones mean to you?' . . . you shall tell them that the waters of the Jordan were cut off before the ark of the covenant of the LORD; when it passed over the Jordan, the waters of the Jordan were cut off. . . . So these stones shall be to the people of Israel a memorial forever" (Josh. 4:6-7). The story of the crossing of the Jordan shows a high degree of kinship with that of the Exodus.

12. W. Barnard, *Op een stoel staan,* vol. 1 (Haarlem: Holland, 1978), p. 69.
13. K. A. Deurloo, *Jozua,* p. 18.

The question the children are expected to ask strongly resembles the question asked by the youngest child the night of the Passover: "Why is this night different from all other nights?" The twelve stones are not sacred objects but signs referring to the feet of the priests who stood in position in the midst of the Jordan. The combination of Exodus and entry also occurs in Psalm 114, where again it is clear we are not dealing with a literal account.

Also, the sequel in the book of Joshua is liturgical in nature. The crossing of the Jordan took place precisely three days before the celebration of the Passover. But the Passover may only be celebrated by those who belong to the covenant, that is, those who are circumcised (Ex. 12:43f.). In the time of wilderness wanderings this had been neglected, but now the people have three days in which to have themselves circumcised in order to be able to celebrate the Passover (Josh. 5).

For the first time the feast is celebrated in the land of Canaan; for the first time it is celebrated with the yield of that land. On that very day the manna stopped. They ate without having sown, an allusion to the year of the Sabbath or to the Year of Jubilee (Lev. 25:11, 12). The theme of seven times seven that shines through the story plays a role in the fall of Jericho, while it also serves as a description for the period between Passover and the Feast of Weeks. The Year of Jubilee echoes the fact that the land was a gift. The people were allowed to receive it as God's gift, something very different from having to conquer it by one's own strength.

What we have here is prophetic narrative, a narrative whose focus is on the future, as is true for all commemoration or celebration in the Bible. Jericho now becomes representative for the whole land given to Israel. There is no siege in the normal sense: instead there is a liturgical procession led by the ark of the covenant while seven priests carry seven rams' horns (the trumpets of jubilee) before the ark. At the sound of those trumpets the people raise a great shout, and the walls of Jericho collapse. The word used for the shouting also occurs in the temple liturgy in Psalm 89:16-17:

Blessed are the people who know the festal shout,
who walk, O LORD, in the light of thy countenance,
who exult in thy name all the day,
and extol thy righteousness.

At Jericho the priests headed the procession. The action could not have been more liturgical. Following the act of taking possession of the land, the land symbolically represented by Jericho and Ai, there is mention of a liturgical conclusion (Josh. 8:30-35). Joshua built an altar. Facing that altar on which sacrifices are offered are the people with the ark and the priests in the midst. Joshua reads the words of the Torah to them — a liturgical pattern of events, says Deurloo, that is typical for the temple in Jerusalem.

The book of Joshua closes with the covenant renewal at Shechem that begins with a grand recital of the saving acts of God. This act of commemoration issues in the call to choose — now: serve the Lord or serve strange gods. And the people answered: "We also will serve the LORD, for he is our God" (Josh. 24:18). The covenant was renewed, and as a sign a large stone was set up at Shechem "under the oak in the sanctuary of the LORD" (v. 26).

Probably the most pronounced example of a liturgically conditioned book in the Bible is Deuteronomy, a book that also occupied a central place in the life of the early Christians. It is quoted no fewer than 190 times in the New Testament. A familiar example of this is the story of the temptation of Jesus in the wilderness (Matt. 4:1-11), a story in which texts from Deuteronomy are pivotal. In this connection we cannot fail to mention the so-called "travel section" in Luke (9:51–18:14), material that does not occur in the other Gospels and that completely follows the order of Deuteronomy.[14] In Deuteronomy celebrating and learning form a unity. "Does not precisely the book of Deuteronomy, as we now know and read it, direct our attention to the

14. J. Wijngaards, *Deuteronomium: uit de grondtekst vertaald en uitgelegd* (Roermond: Romen, 1971), intro., sec. 9.

unity of celebration and instruction, on the true delight in the law (Torah) which embraces both?"[15] Once every seven years, at the Feast of Booths, says Deuteronomy 31:10, the central part of this book (chaps. 4–30) must be read to the people. This section of the book was originally divided into 22 parts which probably correspond with the 22 strophes of Psalm 119, the psalm that celebrates the praise of the Torah. This covenant instruction probably took place in Succoth east of the Jordan. The subdivisions are the telling and reexperiencing of Israel's salvation history (5:1–11:32) in conjunction with which the people were exhorted to remain faithful, the proclamation and explanation of the laws (12:1–26:15), and the renewal of the covenant (26:16-19). Subsequently the people, with the ark of the covenant, walked in procession through the Jordan to Shechem to ratify the covenant while hearing blessings and curses pronounced.

Deuteronomy shows us also that Israel took over a variety of practices from Canaanite worship: pilgrim festivals, the giving of tithes, the sacrificial rights of priests, the consecration of the firstborn, leaving the last sheaf in the field, and so on. These practices were reinterpreted from within Israel's religious framework while the Canaanite religion as such was vehemently opposed.[16]

Having seen how important the liturgical viewpoint is for the interpretation of the Bible, we must now raise the question how all this functioned in biblical times. Although the data are fragmentary, it is clear in any case that the Sabbath and the feasts were pivotal. Another important question concerns the role of the temple and the synagogue. But we should first pause to consider the unity of the Bible and the fundamental significance of "remembering."

---

15. S. L. S. de Vries, "Deuteronomium: Vredesvoorwaarden voor Mokum," *De eerste dag* V, 4 (1982): 3ff. (a publication of the Council of Churches in the Netherlands).
16. See J. Wijngaards, *Deuteronomium*, intro., sec. 3.

2. The Unity of the Bible

As noted earlier, the Tanak has a concentric structure consisting of Torah, Prophets, and Writings, with the Torah at the center. In the Torah the mighty acts of God are described. The prophets summon people to remember the acts of God — that is, to act in accordance with the Torah and to apply the directions of the Torah to the situations of daily life. The Writings reflect the more personal and individual reactions to the Torah. These reactions show much variety — all the way from the relativizing and sceptical reflections of Ecclesiastes to the visions of Daniel, who is not classed with the prophets.

Christians often find it hard to accept the centrality of the Torah because of their belief that many of its precepts are antiquated. Given this belief, the book of Leviticus remains a closed book. But this is a serious misunderstanding. True, the literal meaning of the precepts has usually been superseded. But much more is at stake.

Take the example of leprosy, for which Leviticus 13 offers a long list of regulations. Commenting on this matter, J. van der Werf remarks:

> We discover here, not merely a number of very desirable (for that time) and wise rules, but something else: the fact that attention is given to leprosy. A leper, we are told, is unclean. This means not only that the leper is medically dangerous but theologically anomalous. In the promised land God has in mind, in the society as God intends it, only the unblemished, the sound person fits in — the person of whom God can say: "good" as he said of the creation on the sixth day. A person must be sound, not only spiritually but also physically. It is for good reason that the future vision of Isaiah 35 pictures a world in which no unclean person will be seen. According to Matthew, Jesus' first sign was the healing of a leper (Matt. 8). In other words, also these legal prescriptions give us Torah, even when in themselves they are passé as far as we are concerned.[17]

17. J. van der Werf, *Oefeningen in het leerhuis* (Amersfoort: Roelofs van Goor, 1966), p. 35.

Scripture is one and as such it testifies to God's action in history. But what of the New Testament? Again, one may discern a concentric structure.[18] The heart of it, the new Torah, is the Gospels, while the letters (like the Prophets in the Tanak) exhort the church to live in accordance with the new Torah — to "remember" the Gospels. Revelation is then to be understood as a "writing."

The most important question that must be raised at this point concerns the relationship between the Old and the New Testament. The heart of the answer to that question is that the unity of the two testaments is anchored in the person of Jesus Christ. From the Gospels we know that Jesus lived by the Torah. He kept the Sabbath, attended the synagogue, observed the feasts, and studied the Torah.[19] "Think not that I have come to abolish the law and the prophets; I have come not to abolish them, but to fulfill them" (Matt. 5:17). To "fulfill" here means "to restore again," "to restore to its original purpose and intent." The text, incidentally, also reflects the fidelity of the Jewish Christian churches to the Torah. Jesus here places himself in tradition — with fresh accents, to be sure, but that is typical for rabbinical Judaism. It knows both continuity and renewal — continuity, because the instruction of Moses remains the authoritative point of departure, and renewal because life is in flux and new experiences must be accounted for in interpretation. In the history of the church, one observes that the newness of Jesus' preaching was increasingly emphasized at the expense of the continuity.[20]

With reference to the relationship between the Old and the New Testament, the popular scheme of prediction and "fulfilment" (or coming true) does not make sense. Viewing the Old Testament as a sort of preamble to the New fails to do justice to the unity of Scripture. Miskotte, following Karl Barth, speaks of the Old Testament as testimony to the time of expec-

---

18. Ibid.
19. D. Flusser, *Jesus,* 3rd ed. (Bussum: de Haan, 1979).
20. P. J. Tomson, "Gaaf zal je zijn, zoals je hemelse Vader gaaf is," in *Geliefd is de mens* (Neukirchen-Vluyn: Neukirchener Verlag, 1981).

tation and of the New as testimony to the time of remembrance.[21] Both are directed to the same name, the same event, the same salvation, and both are equally distant from the center of revelation.

The unity that embraces both "testimonies" is evident from the numerous Old Testament citations, terms, and concepts that permeate the New. One could call the New Testament a continuous interpretation of the Old with some new accents. It is precisely these interpretations which, as we shall see later, play a large role in the liturgy, particularly the liturgy of the feasts.

The problematic character of the idea of "prediction" can best be illustrated by way of the texts from Isaiah read in the churches around Christmas and Easter — namely, selections from chapter 9 and chapter 53. With regard to Isaiah 53, in the period before Easter it must be said that the Old Testament does not know of the figure of the suffering Messiah. The familiar text concerning the suffering servant was not a messianic text in Israel. The expression "suffering servant" may refer inter alia to Israel or to a prophet. Luke 24:27 (the interpretation of the Scriptures to the disciples of Emmaus) does not speak of the "coming true" of a prediction but of the fact that Jesus, looking back, saw in the suffering servant the pattern of his own life. He presents a new interpretation of the text, offering a new content. The prophetic word can always and again enter a new phase of fulfilment. That is the basic pattern of all prophetic speech in the Bible. Something similar applies to Isaiah 9, where we are told that "to us a child is born, to us a son is given" (v. 6). The reference here is not to a child but to a king. We find the same sort of language in Psalm 2. Of this, too, it must be said that only later did people in the church relate this text to the coming of Jesus. Jesus himself never made the connection. Let me cite Van der Werf again: "The words of the Old Testament must be examined again and again to discover their intent

21. K. H. Miskotte, *When the Gods are Silent* (New York: Harper and Row, 1967), pp. 113-116.

but at the same time one must remember that they contain a residue of unknown possibilities. Mary can look over Hannah's shoulder for the words of the Magnificat; the story of Joshua gets its own peculiar fulfilment in the life of the New Joshua (= Jesus); the contours of the true messianic king can never be discovered without knowledge of Saul, David, and Solomon. Jesus takes the entire message of the Old Testament and rewrites it in the history of his own life."[22]

Perhaps greater clarity can be achieved by speaking of a double perspective.[23] One perspective looks from the Old Testament to the New and regards Christ as the fulfilment of the Law and the Prophets; another looks from the New to the Old and regards the Law and the Prophets as prefigurations of Christ (which is something other than prediction). The Old Testament sheds light on how we are to view Jesus but Jesus at the same time makes clear the intent of the Law and the Prophets. The first perspective is embodied in John 1:45: "We have found him of whom Moses in the law and also the prophets wrote"; the second is in John 1:17: "For the law was given through Moses; grace and truth came through Jesus Christ." The unity of Scripture given in this double perspective is fundamental in every act of remembering and in every celebration of the acts of God.

3. Remembrance

In the Bible, all that is created, human beings in particular, are called to praise. In biblical terms this means the celebration of the mighty acts of God. Over and over, when this celebration is in view, there is reference to remembering or remembrance or anamnesis. The Hebrew word for remembrance, *zakar*, has as its fundamental meaning "to be mindful of" with the added

22. J. van der Werf, *Oefeningen*, p. 43.
23. W. G. Overbosch, "Kroniek," in *Mededelingen van de Prof. dr. G. van der Leeuwstichting,* instalment 55 (Amsterdam, 1970), pp. 4369ff.

15

implication of "calling on," "invoking," "moving to action"; hence it is dynamic in nature.[24] The term "remembering" suggests a linking of past and present; by it the past is made present again in the here and now.

It is important to make a distinction between an act of the intellect by which one returns mentally to the past and the reverse process by which the past is re-presented and brought into the present, where it becomes active again and renews the impulse to act. Remembrance, or "memorializing," is an activity that is not restricted to the intellect but that involves the whole person who is moved to action by this reenactment of the past. Remembrance is inseparable from action. In many places in the Bible we read that God remembered his people. This remembering always entails his saving action. When God remembers his people in distress, then a rescue operation is about to be staged. Consider these examples:

"So it was that, when God destroyed the cities of the valley, God remembered Abraham, and sent Lot out of the midst of the overthrow" (Gen. 19:29).

"And God heard their groaning, and God remembered his covenant with Abraham, with Isaac, and with Jacob. And God saw the people of Israel, and God knew their condition" (Ex. 2:24-25).

"Arise, call upon your god! Perhaps the god will give a thought to us, that we do not perish" (Jon. 1:6).

The word "remember" also occurs in the New Testament. We all know the statement uttered by the criminal crucified next to Jesus: "Jesus, remember me when you come in your kingly power" (Luke 23:42).

Corresponding to this act of remembering by God there is the remembrance of God's acts by human beings. This also is not a mere intellectual act of recall but the act of entering into relationship with that God whose earlier deeds imply a promise

24. R. Boon, "De joodse wortels van de christelijke eredienst," chap. 2, *Mededelingen van de Prof. dr. G. van der Leeuwstichting,* instalment 40 (Amsterdam, 1970).

for the present. Van der Werf offers this concise formulation. "Then and there God acted thus, and because it is he who then and there acted thus, the believing community may know that also now in our present situation he will act thus."[25] This is clearly expressed in Deuteronomy 5:2-4: "The LORD our God made a covenant with us in Horeb. Not with our fathers did the LORD make this covenant, but with us, who are all of us here alive this day. The LORD spoke with you face to face at the mountain, out of the midst of the fire." The story that is ever repeated afresh remains decisively significant for future generations. On the basis of God's faithfulness, as Psalm 132 expresses it, his salvation may also be expected in the future.

It is not surprising that in such a liturgical book as Deuteronomy the call to remembrance should be sounded twelve times. Remembrance is especially prominent in the celebration of Passover. Every generation in Israel may and will say anew: "And the Egyptians treated us harshly, and afflicted us, and laid upon us hard bondage. Then we cried to the LORD the God of our fathers, and the LORD heard our voice, and saw our affliction, our toil, and our oppression; and the LORD brought us out of Egypt with a mighty hand and an outstretched arm, with great terror, with signs and wonders, and he brought us into this place and gave us this land, a land flowing with milk and honey" (Deut. 26:6-9).

Remembering God's saving acts leads to singing about these acts, to the praise of the name of him who performed these acts. God's acts must be celebrated.

I will call to mind the deeds of the LORD;
yea, I will remember thy wonders of old. (Ps. 77:11)

Against this background one can also speak of God as the holy One who is "enthroned on the praises of Israel" (Ps. 22:3).

We also find this remembrance or anamnesis in Paul's statement on the institution of the Lord's Supper in which Jesus

25. J. van der Werf, *Oefeningen*, p. 46.

is quoted as saying: "Do this in remembrance of me." At issue here is not an act of memory, a recalling of something that happened in the past. At issue is a living relationship, a concern to be re-engrossed by his deeds. In other words, to remember Christ means to follow him, to act in his spirit. In the remembrance of the Eucharist past and future come together in the present, we are united with the risen Lord, and he is with us to the close of the age.

"The celebration of the Eucharist, in all of its historical vibrancy, is full of promise for the future. It inspires us to work for the coming of the Kingdom and to look forward to the return of the Lord: the moment when the mirror of symbol and rite — a mirror which here remains for ever blurred and hazy no matter what — will cease to exist."[26]

Although the Eucharist is an important focus in the New Testament liturgy, it is not the only place in worship where remembrance occurs. It happens when the Scriptures are read in the services of temple, synagogue, and church. Again, it is not matters of historical interest which constitute the central focus but the proclamation of God's action in its significance for the present and the future. In this remembrance, as has been correctly pointed out, the worshippers' attention is riveted upon "God's speech and action in the world of man" and not on the psychological aspects of the remembering person.[27] (However, biblical remembering presupposes a kind of anthropological-psychological structure which is at odds with the sense of life of modern people in the West. See chapter 3 for further discussion.)

Mainly at stake in the remembering that constitutes the core of all liturgical celebration are "the demonstrations of God's redemptive purpose which, though they took place in the past, are understood and experienced, confessed and interpreted, liturgically in the present in such a way that their continuing power to liberate, redeem, and reconcile is made man-

26. G. Lukken, *De onvervangbare weg van de liturgie* (Hilversum: Gooi en Sticht, 1980).
27. R. Boon, in *Mededelingen*, p. 31 n. 4.

ifest for the present and the future."[28] Corresponding with this reality is the fact that many parts of the Bible are rendered in the present tense. The Bible is primarily intended to function in the liturgy as a text to be read aloud. The purpose is that those who hear it are personally addressed in the concreteness of their existence. The liturgy is here "the point of intersection" of the ages, "the point of contact" for the consummation of history on earth, and "a window" open toward the coming kingdom of God.[29] All this takes place in our history in the present dispensation and is not a kind of participation, by way of certain rituals, in a prehistoric myth.

In this connection it is often said that biblical thought and therefore biblical remembrance is characterized by a linear notion of time. The cyclical view of time dominant in archaic cultures was definitely left behind in the Bible. A salvation history unfolds from creation to consummation. The tendency at this point is to equate the modern linear concept of time with the biblical redemptive-historical concept of time. In the linear idea of time the past has definitely been left behind and the future has not yet arrived. The present is like a spot of light that moves from the past to the future but nevertheless remains in isolation from that future. However, the biblical notion of time may not be equated either with the modern linear concept or with the cyclical concept of the world of myth. In the biblical world a forward movement is at work, a redemptive-historical dynamic; but one can also find cyclical components. Day and night, the months and the seasons of the year, the years themselves — all are subject to repetition. The very word for "year" in the Old Testament means "change" or "repetition." In sum, the biblical notion of time has both linear and cyclical components.

In this connection Lammens has remarked that the biblical notion of remembrance rests on two foundational facts.[30]

28. Ibid.
29. Ibid.
30. G. N. Lammens, "Het kerkelijk jaar en de liturgische jaarorde," *De eerste dag* 1 (1977), instalment 1.

There is (a) the historic character of the redemptive event and (b) the rhythmic nature of the passage of time. Forward-moving history, the returning weeks and revolving seasons, together form an "escalator-like" movement in time (the term was coined by W. Barnard). Remembrance is rooted in this structure. Again and again there are "new processions in time having the same points from which to look back." We also may recall here the saying of Baal Shem Tov: "Forgetfulness leads to exile; remembrance is the secret of redemption." In remembrance the celebrant is involved in the secret of redemption, an involvement which, as Deuteronomy shows, is of fundamental importance for responsible action.

4. The Language of Images

The secret of redemption, the completion of God's work of creation, cannot be expressed in ordinary, everyday language because it concerns matters that far surpass our capacity to understand. The language in which the biblical authors wrote down their testimonies — their experiences with "the living speech of God" — is the language of the faith community which dreams dreams and sees visions and lives by expectation. But if we now say that the language of the Bible is the language of symbolism we must be immediately alert to the misunderstandings that lie in wait for us. To begin with, authentic language is always symbolic ("symbolic" in the sense of groping for the inexpressible, a referring to inexhaustible riches of meaning). This means we must guard against saying "this is only symbolic," as though that meant "this is not real." That is a fatal misunderstanding in modern Western thought. Nor is the use of symbolic language something for an earlier stage in life, the stage of children or underdeveloped people which we have left behind.

Divine things can only be expressed in images and symbols, not in abstract concepts. We are here touching upon problems associated with the question concerning the relationship between symbol and reality. It is characteristic of modern

20

thought that it has driven a wedge between symbol and reality, placing the two in opposition. Generally speaking, there have been two major sets of reactions to this separation where it concerns symbol and reality in the Bible: modernism and fundamentalism. Modernism crosses out reality and turns the symbol into an idea (only what a photographer can capture on film is true). Fundamentalism views symbol and reality as concurrent or identical, or at least so it seems. But in reality the symbol is crossed out.

In this respect modernism and fundamentalism, remarkably enough, share a common thought pattern. For both of them the symbolic is unreal; both substitute for it a positivistic criterion which regards as true only that which is observable by the senses.

But the Bible — and its language — does not know of any such reductionist model of reality. Reality in the Bible is symbolic: it far exceeds and transcends what we moderns describe with terms and phrases like "historical," "really happened," "empirical reality," and the like.

The language in which the Bible is written, an idiom in which reality is symbolic reality, can best be described as mythical. Of course, by using here the word "mythical," one opens the door to a host of misunderstandings. Mythical — as J. M. de Jong has stated (and in the sections which follow we shall reproduce in outline what he has to say[31]), has a different connotation than "myth," and "myth" again has a different "feel" than "mythology." In myth, primeval events outside of time come alive again when actualized by means of ritual. Myth provides the foundation for the reality of everyday; or, as Van Baaren puts it, myth is "the sacred story of primeval events which still underlie the present and open a perspective on the future."[32] Narrating the myth, therefore, is a sacral happening that may only be staged on solemn occasions.

31. J. M. de Jong: "De taal van de bijbel en onze levenswerkelijkheid, in *Voorrang aan de Joekomst* (Nijkerk: Callenbach, 1909), pp. 15-40.
32. Th. van Baaren, *Uit de wereld der religie,* cited in his *Wij mensen* (Utrecht: Bijleveld, 1960), p. 185.

In this sense the Bible has no myths. In fact, reality in Scripture is demythologized. A well-known example is the first creation story (Gen. 1:1–2:4a) in which the cosmos is demythologized. Sun, moon, and stars — divine powers in the ancient cultures — here become celestial bodies serving as lights in the firmament to separate day and night "for signs and for seasons" (Gen. 1:14). There is here an underlying polemic against a Babylonian worldview. Something similar is present in the so-called throne chariot vision of Ezekiel (1:4-28) in which the entire cosmos, which Babylonian thought peopled with celestial gods (stars), forms the throne chariot of God. The four living creatures of Ezekiel 1:5ff. return in Revelation 4, where they never cease to sing, "Holy, holy, holy is the Lord God Almighty, who was, and is, and is to come." The cosmos which had been worshipped as divine is again reduced to the status of a created thing.

In ancient Greece, also, there is a breakthrough: under the impact of slowly developing thought processes myth becomes mythology, a history of the gods, a speculative and artistic story, a starting point for further reflection. In Israel myth dissolves in consequence of the adoration of the living God, creator and liberator. However, the language the Bible uses comes from the world of myth. For that matter, all living language has a mythical aspect.

We have at our disposal but one language — though it operates on different levels — for referring to and describing the concrete things of the visible world as well as the powers of life and death, beauty and glory — "penultimate" forces within the created world which to believers are referents to God. Hence the powers themselves are not denied, but before God they have no independent status; they lose their omnipotence. As realities of human life these powers can only be referred to in mythical, poetic, and prophetic language. It is the language we need when the subject is love or peace, freedom and justice, life and death. It is mythical, but not mythological, for the myth has been broken not only by reason (Tillich) but also by the witness of the Bible, which replaced myth with liberating action. At this juncture De Jong refers to the narrow

22

road between fundamentalism and modernism that modern people must travel, "for the reality and action of the living God are of another order of being than that of things and ideas." One must constantly keep in mind, however, that no language exists to enable us to describe the action of God with total adequacy. Our best efforts are a groping toward the mystery — the hearing of an echo, seeing a flash of light on the horizon. The name of God is inexpressible.

God nevertheless chose to address us in mythical language, a fact of enormous significance because the language of everyday and that of the world of scientific description are struck dumb when it concerns matters of life and death, liberation and reconciliation, love and justice. Accordingly, the witness of the Bible is the proclamation of the living God in narrative form and mythical language. One must not be too easily frightened by the term "mythical": the negative sound of the word is a product of the eighteenth- and nineteenth-century science of religion which had little understanding of what is typical for biblical thought and language.

In order to understand the Bible correctly we need another way of looking at it, a different perceptual training than any currently in use. This is especially manifest when questions are raised concerning the nature and meaning of miracles. On this subject De Jong states the following:

"When approaching the way the Bible speaks about miracle one should ideally be able to banish from one's mind all terminology derived from the concept of nature. For in the mythical-historical language of the Bible miracles are not oriented to natural law and causality but to the mystery, power and glory of events in which God appears and by which he takes possession of me." This is the sense in which we could possibly interpret Ricoeur when he asserts that though we must *demythologize* (that is, not take myth literally), we must not *demythicize* (throw away the myth).[33] According to Ricoeur, the mythical

33. Quoted by H. M. M. Fortmann, *Als ziende de onzienlijke*, vol. 1 (Hilversum: Gooi en Sticht, 1974), p. 547.

story remains indispensable because it is a symbol that invites further thought. The story merely suggests the hidden meaning; further interpretation is needed. The speaking snake of Genesis 3 did not "really" exist, but we must hold on to the story because the snake has something to tell us. In all this the truth is that one cannot give universally valid answers to the many questions that come up: the diversity within Scripture is just too big.

Mythical language is a language of images, the language of story. That which must be told can often only be told in the form of a story. At the same time one has to say that the story is never finished — it can always be continued. The core of the story can never be completely explained. Besides, the stories of the Bible do not occur in isolation; they constitute a whole and presuppose each other. In a sense, in every story and in every image the whole is present, and hence in that sense every story is exemplary.[34] Nevertheless, all the stories together in no way exhaust their subject, God's action in history.

If then the witness of people to God's action in history is wrapped in stories, images, and symbols, the question raised is (we touched on it in the preceding), Just what is the onto-logical content of these symbols? We found that neither fun-damentalism nor modernism offered us a passable road on which to go. Can we say anything further about "the narrow way" referred to by De Jong?

In the first place, it is good to observe that the wall sep-arating story and reality, story and history, is much thinner than we are inclined to assume. A fact "by itself" is a theoretical abstraction. "Facts" always presuppose values. Human inter-action with reality occurs within the framework of a "story," of a view of life, of accumulated experiences. For that reason there can never be an absolute contrast between story and reality. They do not coincide, nor do people exhaust themselves in their "stories." But story is bound to reality by a thousand threads. The language, with the symbols contained in it, is the medium of interaction with reality about us; hence a story can

34. J. Kuin, *Theologie en literatuur* (Streven, 1980), pp. 33, 575-85.

say something significant about reality. The story, far from being a betrayal of reality, brings its peculiar significance to light. Perhaps one could even speak of an intensification of reality by means of story.

It was, says Kuin, a peculiar reaction to modernism that people, inspired by fear, sought refuge in the so-called "historical facts," which were allegedly much more important than the story. Although this was unintentional, it constituted a surrender to positivism.

In the approach we have chosen to follow, story and symbol are not independent, self-contained entities, nor are they the last word. They witness and refer to immediate experience. Mysticism has often asserted that in the direct encounter with God the story is superfluous. But that is not the case. "Even when the beloved is present the poetry of love has a place and makes sense." For us, people whose faith has not yet turned into sight, those images and stories are an absolute necessity — not, to be sure, as completed systems but as stories that must be handed down. It is essential to learn how succeeding generations of believers have understood and lived with the biblical stories, what things, new and old, they have heard in them.

The watertight division that people in Reformation circles have posited between Bible and tradition is not as valid as at first blush it appears to be. It betrays the influence of the theoretical thought developed in Rationalism and the Enlightenment, which operated with absolute concepts and closed systems. It is the kind of thought that has become blind to images and stories and seeks to lay down meanings once and for all without ambiguity.

In a centuries-long process, observes O. Jager, the images of the Bible have hardened into concepts. "If we act as if the Scriptures only make us think we can no longer discover what it is the Scriptures give us to think." "Living images lead to thoughts but thoughts do not lead to living images" (Checkov, quoted by Jager).[35]

35. O. Jager, *Opklaring* (Ede: Zomer en Keuning, 1980), pp. 7-8.

5. Biblical Symbols

Well, what are the images through which the Bible speaks? In view of the enormous volume of material, we can only mention a few of the main ones. The most important category of biblical images is that of symbols. I shall first offer a few examples from the biblical dictionary of images and symbols by Lurker.[36]

As a preliminary approach to the term "symbol," let us call it "an observable sign by which an experience of the transcendent is expressed." A symbol in the nature of the case does not permit definition. It represents a reality other than the directly visible, at least other than reality as usually interpreted. Within the framework of the Bible the whole of reality is symbolic in the sense that all of creation points to the Creator. As a rule, symbols possess a certain ambiguity, a bipolarity. They can hint at life as well as death, good as well as evil. The serpent of Genesis 3 brought death; the bronze serpent in the wilderness gave life. The primeval water of Genesis 1 that represented the powers of chaos and hence of death in Genesis 2:10 becomes the water of life that waters the garden. The water that in the story of the flood enters the cosmos, again, is the power of chaos and evil to which human beings succumb because they bring these powers down upon themselves. Water means menace and death. It returns in many places: the water of the Red Sea, the water of the river of death, the water of baptism. We are buried with Christ in baptism, submerged in the water of death, in order to rise from it again; thus the water of baptism conveys new life.

The book of Revelation refers to "the river of the water of life, bright as crystal, flowing from the throne of God and of the Lamb through the middle of the street of the city; also, on either side of the river, the tree of life with its twelve kinds of fruit, yielding its fruit each month" (Rev. 22:1-2, incorporating the symbolism of Ezek. 47). In the chapter before, we read that

---

36. M. Lurker, *Woordenboek van bijbelse beelden en symbolen* (Boxtel: Katholieke, 1975).

"the sea was no more." The powers of chaos and evil have been removed. Hence water is a very rich symbol in which the bipolar nature of symbols is clearly shown.

In addition to water, many other ordinary things in the Bible are deeply symbolic in meaning. We shall now discuss in order the following: the wilderness and the number forty associated with it, mountains, bread and wine, light, salt, incense, myrrh, myrtle, and the sound of the shofar.

The *wilderness* is the region of death, the opposite of inhabitable and fruitful land. It represents the experience of being tested; it images the period of preparation. Jesus fasted and remained in the wilderness forty days and forty nights. At the end of this period he was tempted by the devil. The *number forty* has a wealth of associations. In the account of the flood it rained for forty days and nights. Moses stayed in the mountain forty days and forty nights. Elijah walked forty days and forty nights through the wilderness to Mt. Horeb. Whereas the wilderness is the place of trial, the number forty suggests a period of trial.

Israel's journey over forty years through the wilderness becomes the picture of God's people travelling through the world on their way to the Promised Land.

The *mountain*, often occurring in combination with the previous two images, is the image of revelation. On Mt. Moriah, later the temple mountain (2 Chron. 3:1), God revealed himself to Abraham, as he did to Moses on Mt. Sinai and later to Elijah. In a vision Isaiah sees the nations "flowing" to the temple mountain of the Lord (Isa. 2:2-3). Jesus starts his proclamation of the kingdom from a mountain (the Sermon on the Mount), an event that recalls the announcement of the Ten Commandments on Mt. Sinai. Jesus' transfiguration occurred on Mt. Tabor, as did the appearance of Moses and Elijah with him as symbols of Torah and the Prophets.

Bread and *wine* almost speak for themselves. In the celebration of the Eucharist they first of all depict, as the work of our hands, our existence brought in as an offering and an act of self-surrender. Then, from the hands of our Lord, we receive

27

that life, the blessed life, back again in the form of bread and wine — both as images of communion with the Lord and fellowship with one another, the body of Christ. The wine is at the same time an image of the blood that was shed, an image that has eschatological significance: "I tell you I shall not drink again of this fruit of the vine until that day when I drink it new with you in my Father's kingdom" (Matt. 26:29). Wine is closely associated with the messianic future. Isaiah speaks of the Lord who on his mountain will prepare for the nations a banquet with the finest of foods and the most splendid of wines (Isa. 25:6). Jesus' first act of public ministry was changing water into wine at a wedding. The water taken from purification jars — the water of the Torah — was made into wine. In connection with the miraculous feeding of the five thousand (John 6:1-15), Jesus said: "I am the bread of life; he who comes to me shall not hunger" (6:35). This same theme of eating, of sharing, and having bread to spare occurs already in the stories about the prophet Elisha. There, too, we read of a limited quantity of food that, on instructions from Elisha, has to serve a hundred men. After his servant protests that there is too little, Elisha says: "Give them to the men that they may eat, for thus says the LORD, 'They shall eat and have some left' . . . and they ate, and had some left, according to the Word of the LORD" (2 Kings 4:42-44).

Light is a reference to God, who is clothed in a garment of light (Ps. 104:2). It also has messianic significance: "The people who walked in darkness have seen a great light" (Isa. 9:2). God himself is light. In the new Jerusalem the sun and the moon will no longer be needed, "for the glory of God is its light, and its lamp is the Lamb" (Rev. 21:23). "By its light shall the nations walk" (v. 24). Light has to do with insight and truth. "Thy word is a lamp to my feet and a light to my path" (Ps. 119:105). Well known also is the symbolism of light in the Gospel of John. One might get the impression that the biblical symbols are exclusively visual in nature. That is not so, though the visual does dominate. But the image of wine, for example, is not only visual; it also has associations of taste and smell.

Salt is a symbol of durability, of life-preserving power, of the firmness of the covenant. "It is a covenant of salt forever before the LORD for you and for your offspring with you" (Num. 18:19). The background here is the fact that all cereal offerings had to be seasoned with salt (Lev. 2:13). Again, the bipolar character of the symbol is evident. Salt can stand for life as well as death and corruption. Elisha makes the water wholesome by throwing salt in it (2 Kings 2:19-22), but in Psalm 107:33-34 we read: "He turns rivers into a desert . . . a fruitful land into a salty waste, because of the wickedness of its inhabitants." It can be either the salt of the covenant or the salt of destruction. In the New Testament, spirit, peace, and humor all form part of the symbolism of salt: "You are the salt of the earth" (Matt. 5:13). "Have salt in yourselves, and be at peace with one another" (Mark 9:50). "Let your speech always be gracious, seasoned with salt, so that you may know how you ought to answer everyone" (Col. 4:6).

Smells too may have symbolic value. Incense, for example, is a symbol of adoration. "Let my prayer be counted as incense before thee, and the lifting up of my hands as an evening sacrifice!" (Ps. 141:2). Revelation mentions "golden bowls full of incense," the prayers of the saints (Rev. 5:8). And in Revelation 8:4 we read: "And the smoke of the incense rose with the prayers of the saints from the hand of the angel before God." Incense also has messianic meaning. "All those from Sheba shall come. They shall bring gold and frankincense" (Isa. 60:6). Besides incense, myrrh also belongs to the gifts fit for a king. In the Old Testament, incense and myrrh are the attributes of a royal bridegroom. "What is that coming up from the wilderness, like a column of smoke, perfumed with myrrh and frankincense, with all the fragrant powders of the merchant?" (Song of Sol. 3:6) They are the royal fragrances of the Messiah and of Paradise. A third source of fragrance with symbolic meaning is the myrtle, of which there are many kinds. In the instructions concerning the celebration of the Feast of Tabernacles (Lev. 23:39), there is special mention of the citrus fruits (the fragrant etrog among them) and a variety of branches which are all to be brought together for the enhancement of the feast. To this number Nehemiah adds the olive, the wild olive, and the myrtle (8:15). The myrtle is the symbol of love and election, as is evident from Isaiah 55:13.

Finally, there is the symbol of sound. In the Bible there is repeated reference to a wind instrument called the *shofar*, an instrument made out of a ram's horn. The word "shofar" is also translated trumpet or horn. The Year of Jubilee begins with the blowing of the shofar on the Day of Atonement (Lev. 25:8-9). The sound of the shofar was intended to attract the attention of God. "On the day of your gladness also, and at your appointed feasts, and at the beginnings of your months, you shall blow the trumpets over your burnt offerings and over the sacrifices of your peace offerings; they shall serve you for remembrance before your God" (Num. 10:10). Still today, on the morning of the Jewish New Year and at the end of the great Day of Atonement, the shofar is blown in the synagogue to bring the people into remembrance before God. Also, the image of the end time is linked with the sound of the shofar. Then, says the prophet Zechariah, "The LORD God will sound the trumpet and march forth" (9:14). And in Paul we read, "For the trumpet will sound, and the dead will be raised imperishable" (1 Cor. 15:52). The motif of the end time also comes through in the words of Jesus: "and he will send out his angels with a loud trumpet call, and they will gather his elect from the four winds, from one end of heaven to the other" (Matt. 24:31).

These are just a few examples of biblical symbols, but enough has been said to get an impression and to proceed further with an inquiry into their nature. In a symbol the image and that which is imaged are very closely bound up with each other, like the figure and its shadow, neither of which can exist without the other.[37] This means that the things around us are more than their appearance, form, and function. And that dimension suggested by the word "more" is the relationship to the Creator, the fact of being caught up in a redemptive-

---

37. R. Boon, in *Mededelingen*, p. 76.

historical perspective. "For the creation was subjected to futility, not of its own will but by the will of him who subjected it in hope; because the creation itself will be set free from its bondage to decay and obtain the glorious liberty of the children of God. We know that the whole creation has been groaning in travail together until now" (Rom. 8:20-22). This dynamic vision of reality, a vision in which all of creation is involved in and focused on the ultimate meaning, goal, and consummation of the created world (cf. the doxologies in which the whole of creation is involved or represented), has practically been lost under Hellenistic influence. Boon puts the problem as follows: "Biblical eschatology was confused with the metaphysics of Greek philosophy. As a result the redemptive-historical notions of the Bible were taken in the direction of ontology."[38]

What is meant is that in Platonic thought the visible is the image of the invisible, to be sure, while the invisible world is the world of eternal, unchanging, true being that can only be grasped by pure intellect. The supersensual world is the perfect archetype of the finite, imperfect, and perishable things of this concrete world.[39] In this understanding of the world there is no room for a redemptive-historical dynamic — for a creation that is on its way to its destination.

If it be true that in a symbol the image and what it signifies are as closely bound up with each other as a figure and its shadow, then a symbol has a revelational character, then it can reveal to us something of the kingdom of God, of God's creative and redemptive action. It does not permit direct vision; it is referential, and we only know by faith, for sight "from face to face" still lies hidden in the future. Still, in faith symbols have real import, import by which one is enabled to participate in the things of the kingdom of God. The symbols make possible our communion with the Lord and with one another as citizens of the kingdom.

In the celebration of the Lord's Supper this becomes very

38. Ibid., p. 78.
39. C. J. de Vogel, *Theoria* (Assen: Van Gorcum, 1967), chap. 7.

31

clear — at least it can be, despite the numerous misunderstandings and misconceptions resulting from the fatal disjunction of
symbol and reality. In bread and wine Christ himself is present,
represented, just as the figure is represented in the shadow.
Thus the water of baptism is symbolic, representative of the
water of creation as the source of all the possibilities of existence, and the Spirit imparts to it his regenerational power.[40]

Summarizing this material, one can say that the whole of
the created cosmos is symbolic, but the most central symbol is
the human being created after the image of God. This means
that he or she is called to represent the Creator in this world.
Yet human beings cannot be equated with the image of God:
being created after the image of God, they are impressions of
the image. It is Christ as the image of God who affords us the
correct insight here. He truly mirrors God's intent. To make
images of God outside of Christ is not permitted to human
beings. The symbol makes present that which is represented.
In this sense Christ is the symbol of God. "He who has seen
me has seen the Father" (John 14:9). We cannot say the same
thing of human beings who are created after the image and in
the likeness of God (Gen. 1:26).[41] Likeness is more derivative
and indirect in relation to that which is imaged. Whereas in the
symbol similarity is accentuated, in likeness there is a note of
dissimilarity.

Symbols constitute the most important category — the
backbone, as it were, of the language of images employed in
the Bible. They are also essential for understanding the linkage
of meaning within Scripture and therefore serve a key role in
exegesis and liturgy. In this respect also much has been lost.

Whereas older, more literal translations of the Bible con-
sistently translated key words in the original by the same word
in the target language, the more modern versions often use
synonyms in the interest of contemporary word usage. Unfor-

40. Thus Tertullian, cited by J. P. de Jong, *De eucharistie* (Hilversum:
Gooi en Sticht, 1966), p. 19.
41. R. Boon, in *Mededelingen*, p. 74.

tunately, the result in many instances is that the deeper meaning and mutual connections are lost. Thus in Ecclesiastes 9:8 we read, "Let your garments be always white; let not oil be lacking on your head" (RSV). The Good News Bible translates: "Always look happy and cheerful." However, the terms "white" and "oil" are key words. The prescribed clothing for those who serve in the sanctuary is white linen. The Ancient of Days in Daniel 7:9 wears clothes that are white as snow. Christ's clothing on the Mount of Transfiguration became "dazzling white." The angels in the tomb were dressed in "dazzling apparel" (Luke 24:4). In Revelation, white is the symbol of perfect purity and glory. Those who have come out of the great tribulation have washed their robes and made them white in the blood of the Lamb (7:13-15). For that reason the color of baptismal clothing in the Christian church was white.

The term *oil* is no less significant. Oil was used in the anointing of priests, kings, and prophets, and it signifies anointing by the Spirit, being consecrated to God. The anointed one par excellence is the Messiah. All these symbolic meanings are echoed in the passage cited from Ecclesiastes, but they are lost when contemporary usage becomes the criterion in translation. (The purpose is good, to bring the Bible *closer* to the people. But the actual effect is the opposite. The only proper way is to bring people closer to the Bible.) The language of the Bible is the language of images, images that transmit the testimonies to God's revelation. "Indeed, he said nothing to them without a parable" (Matt. 13:34). Images, too, are only approximations of this reality, but as such are more adequate than concepts. They presuppose in the listener the faculty of imagination which gives one access to the biblical world (cf. chap. 3, sec. 4).

6. The Sabbath

For the celebration, and remembering, of God's mighty acts the feasts in the Bible are pivotal. Feasts, which take place in time, actually structure its passage. The Bible does not know of time as an abstract concept. Time is thought of in terms of its content, and different times differ in content. Eccleasiastes 3 offers a good example: There is "a time to be born, and a time to die, a time to plant, and a time to pluck up what is planted; a time to kill, and a time to heal." The pivotal moments in the times are the feasts, times filled with the celebration of the acts of God. They constitute the essential components of the structure of time and impart meaning to the whole. In the Bible, feasts are not so much intermittent high points in time; instead, they form the basic structure that sustains the times. Celebrating these feast days means that one participates in the events with which the times of feasting are filled. To celebrate means to find a footing for one's life in the mighty acts of God. The person who remembers these acts, who celebrates and experiences them, will also find that his times are filled by them. Thus one's times are ordered in terms of God's action, so that life again becomes livable. In this ordering of time there are two dominant rhythms, the order of the week and the order of the year, the Sabbath and the festivals. In the present section we shall talk about the Sabbath, in the next about the festivals.

We shall skip the question concerning the historical development of the Sabbath and the influence of other cultures on its origin. The important fact is that in the period of the Exile, the period in which the Tanak originated, the Sabbath was a central feature.

In this connection W. Barnard has written:

> In the days when the sacred stories and songs, precepts and sayings, were brought together in writing and became "Scripture," the teachers of the exile offered *the biblical landscape* as a landscape in which to live and feel at home. You can be in exile and still be at home, ill at ease and still have the taste of peace in your mouth — the mouth which sings the songs, tells the stories, and murmurs the words of Moses. And those teachers (Did they know what they were doing? But we do understand in retrospect; we recognize our own pain and ecstasy), in place of the tangible monumental

temple as a foothold offered a temple in time, an oasis in the wilderness of days. The sabbath became the big consolidation for believers, the place of refreshment and rest, a day of insight and outlook and *that* is valid also for us![42]

The celebration of the Sabbath is marked by three pivotal concerns, points toward which the celebration is directed: creation, liberation, and atonement. The link with creation is forged in Exodus 20:11: "For in six days the LORD made heaven and earth, the sea and all that is in them, and rested the seventh day; therefore the LORD blessed the sabbath day and hallowed it." In Deuteronomy 5:15 the call to liberation is sounded: "You shall remember that you were a servant in the land of Egypt, and the LORD your God brought you out thence with a mighty hand and an outstretched arm; therefore the LORD your God commanded you to keep the sabbath day." Finally, in Leviticus 16:30-31, the linkage with the theme of atonement is established: "For on this day [the great Day of Atonement] shall atonement be made for you, to cleanse you. . . . It is a sabbath of solemn rest to you, and you shall afflict yourselves; it is a statute for ever."

The great Day of Atonement was also called "the sabbath of sabbaths," a name that clearly links the order of the week with the yearly calendar. Man and animal, the whole of creation, everything is involved in the celebration of the Sabbath. "That your ox and your ass may have rest, and the son of your bondmaid, and the alien, may be refreshed" (Ex. 23:12). The distinguishing feature of the Sabbath is not the cessation of work but the fact that it is the sign of the covenant with God and therefore holy. The sanctification of the Sabbath serves the maintenance of the covenant.

"The Sabbath teaches us: it is man's destiny to be God's partner in the work of creation, in creating a world which is very good (as we read following the creation of man, Gen. 1:31). And that is the deep meaning of the statement that the Sabbath

42. W. Barnard, *Binnen de tijd* (Hilversum: Paul Brand, 1964), p. 17.

is a 'statute for ever. It is a sign forever between me and the people of Israel' (Ex. 31:16-17)."[43]

. The Sabbath is the image of completed work and, by extension, a picture of the messianic future, of the consummation of all things, a foretaste of the coming kingdom. In remembering and celebrating the Sabbath all these motives come together.

It is a very telling moment when the woman of the house lights the Sabbath candle at the beginning of the Sabbath. This practice goes back to the beginning of the Christian era. It is to be regarded as an act of remembering that out of darkness God called the light into being just as Israel was saved from death and given new life. The Sabbath light also points to the messianic future. The Sabbath meal, which is rooted in Bible times,[44] as a meal in a biblical setting also suggests messianic associations. In the synagogue the so-called Lecha Dodi, a song of welcome to the Sabbath, is sung. Here are the first, second, and final strophes.

Lecha Dodi
The Sabbath Bride

Refrain:
Come, my beloved, with chorus of praise,
Welcome Bride Sabbath, the Queen of the days.

"Keep and Remember"! — in one Divine Word
He that is One made His will heard;
One is the name of Him, One is the Lord!
    His are the fame and the glory and praise!

Sabbath, to welcome thee, joyous we haste;
Fountain of blessing, from ever thou wast —
First in God's planning, thou fashioned the last,
    Crown of His handiwork, chiefest of days.

---

43. P. J. Tomson, "Zes dagen zul je werken en de zevende dag staken," in *Geliefd is de mens* (Neukirchen-Vluyn: Neukirchener Verlag, 1981), p. 68.
44. Safrai, *Das Jüdische Volk*, chap. 9.

Come in thy joyousness, Crown of thy Lord;
Come, bringing peace to the folk of the Word;
Come where the faithful in gladsome accord,
    Hail thee as Sabbath-Bride, Queen of the days.

Come where the faithful are hymning thy praise;
Come as a bride cometh, Queen of the days!

The question that automatically arises now is the relationship between Sabbath and Sunday. The Greco-Roman world had already taken over the seven-day week from Judaism when Christianity first made its appearance. The church adopted as holy Scripture the Old Testament— the Septuagint —which carried clear directions for the celebration of the Sabbath. Soon, however, so the story usually goes, the so-called ceremonial laws were abolished, among which was the Sabbath commandment. In place of the Sabbath came Sunday as the first day of the week.

However, this account does not square with what we read in the New Testament.[45] The early Christians observed the Sabbath as a matter of course. This was also true of Jesus. His criticism was directed not toward the Sabbath as such, but toward the practices that had grown up around it, a criticism that could also be heard in rabbinical circles. Jesus' statement to the effect that the Sabbath is for man and not man for the Sabbath also occurs in rabbinical writings. It is true that early Christians held their meetings on the first day of the week (Mark 16:2; Acts 20:7), but Sunday was no day of rest. Not till A.D. 321 did Constantine turn Sunday into a kind of day of rest, a measure followed some time later by a prohibition of Sabbath observance.

This must be viewed as an anti-Jewish measure rather than as a consequence of reflection on the Old and New Testament. The result was a belief that on biblical grounds Sunday had taken the place of the Sabbath and therefore, as Calvin thought, for example, the command concerning the seventh day now applied to the first day of the week. This line of

45. P. J. Tomson, in *Geliefd is de mens.*

thought is not tenable. "In our time the awareness has grown that the church cannot validate such pretensions with regard to Judaism" (Tomson).

How the church will now deal with the historical data remains a question.[46]

7. The Festivals

The most important feasts in the Bible began as nature festivals and hence reflect the rhythms of nature, the rhythm of sowing and reaping. The striking thing about these festivals is that they have been historicized — that is, they have received their content and meaning from the history of redemption. Thus, for instance, the festival of the barley harvest became the feast of Passover, the celebration of the Exodus. The festival of the wheat harvest became the Feast of Weeks at which the making of the covenant at Sinai was remembered. Finally, the great harvest festival of the fall (wine and oil) became the Feast of Tabernacles, the feast of remembering the wilderness journey. Not that this process of historicizing replaced the original nature motifs. But these images, derived from processes in nature, were incorporated into the perspective of salvation history. The harvest became a symbol of the consummation of history. In this way the processes of nature acquired a symbolic dimension, or, to formulate this from within a biblical climate of thought, the symbolic dimension of these processes unfolded.

In addition to the three festivals we have mentioned there is reference in Leviticus 23 to the celebration of the great Day of Atonement. After the Exile the Feast of Purim, the celebration of the rescue of the Jews by Esther's mediation, was added, as well as Hanukkah, the feast of the dedication of the temple. The commemoration or the fall of the temple and the Simchat Torah, or the Rejoicing with the Torah, arose still later.

In this chapter we shall only discuss the feasts that occur

46. Ibid.

in the Old Testament — that is, Passover, the Feasts of Weeks, and the Feast of Tabernacles, especially because these feasts are continued, in some form, in the Christian tradition. They are all three of them pilgrim festivals. Three times a year, according to Deuteronomy 16:16, all the males had to appear before the Lord at the central sanctuary, but not with empty hands. In all these feasts the core is a celebration of the covenant between God and his people. It is the heart of every liturgical event.

The institution of the Passover, the festival of the Exodus, is reported in Exodus 12. Even a first reading shows what the nature of this remembrance is: "In this manner you shall eat it: your loins girded, your sandals on your feet, and your staff in your hand; and you shall eat it in haste" (v. 11).

It is a dramatic replay of history, done every year to bring home its meaning for the present. People are to observe it as though they themselves had departed from Egypt in the preceding year, as the instruction for the Seder (the first evening of Pesach) reads. The meal described in Exodus 12 continues as the Seder service to this day ("You shall observe this rite as an ordinance for you and for your sons for ever," Ex. 12:24).

Upon closer scrutiny we discover that there is not one but two feasts woven together in Exodus 12, the Passover and the Feast of Unleavened Bread. For seven days people ate unleavened bread, "the bread of affliction," as a reminder of the haste with which the people had been led out of the country. In earlier times *Pesach*, the killing of the passover lamb, had been a family festival. Next to that was the pilgrim festival of unleavened bread (cf. Deut. 16:16). In the days of King Josiah the two festivals were still separate. The combination of the two festivals stems from a later period, as is evident from Ezekiel 45:21 and from the priestly tradition embodied in Exodus 12.[47]

As much as we know about the observance of the Passover in postbiblical times, we know little about the way it was celebrated in biblical times. In any case, the Hallel, Psalms 113–118

47. R. de Vaux, *Ancient Israel*, vol. 2 (New York: McGraw-Hill, 1965), p. 486.

(to be distinguished from the Great Hallel, Pss. 120–136) was part both of the Passover and of the two other pilgrim festivals. Psalms 113 and 114 were sung before the Passover meal and Psalms 115–118 after it. The statement in Mark 14:26, "And when they had sung a hymn, they went out to the Mount of Olives," refers in all likelihood to the second part of the Hallel. As in all remembering, the celebration of the Passover is oriented to the future. It is "a statute for ever." The promises of redemption and deliverance, as we can read in the prophets, remain valid. Thus the observance of Passover gained messianic features. Standing in this tradition Jesus renewed the Passover celebration, realizing its original intent. With him serving as the Passover lamb, the messianic age dawns. When after the resurrection Jesus ate with his disciples (Luke 24:30), the kingdom of God broke through. The eucharistic meal Jesus instituted in remembrance of himself and celebrated with his followers is a meal of redemption.

The Feast of Weeks, the feast of the firstfruits of the harvest, is celebrated seven weeks after Passover on the fiftieth day. Two loaves of bread made of fresh wheat flour are to be offered to God as firstfruits. In the instructions for this festival the provision for the poor and for the stranger is striking: "When you reap the harvest of your land, you shall not reap your field to its very border, nor shall you gather the gleanings after the harvest; you shall leave them for the poor and for the stranger: I am the LORD your God" (Lev. 23:15-22). To celebrate, to remember, without doing justice is an impossibility: the one implies the other. Where the two are separated, the celebration loses its meaning and perspective, and, as Amos shows, becomes a mockery. This feast, later than Passover, was also linked with salvation history, in this case with the establishment of the covenant of Sinai, although there is no explicit mention of this in the Old Testament. It is mentioned in passing in the deuterocanonical writings (2 Maccabees 12:31-32 and Tobit 2:1) and only became the feast of the giving of the Torah in rabbinical Judaism.[48]

48. P. J. Tomson, in *Geliefd is de mens*, pp. 443ff.

As for the Christian feast of Pentecost, as described in the book of Acts, though no connections were made with the events at Sinai it cannot be an accident that the Spirit was poured out precisely on the Feast of Weeks (Shavuot). At Pentecost there was a bursting of boundaries: salvation is for all nations, as the prophets had said. The theme of the universality of salvation plays a role both in the Jewish and in the Christian feast of Pentecost. This universalism surfaces at least in a certain branch of Judaism in the period of the second temple. An expression of it can be found in the linkage of the Feast of Weeks with the commemoration of the covenant with Noah. In both Jewish and Christian traditions Psalm 104 acquired a place in the celebration.

[Thou] makest the winds thy messengers, fire and flame thy ministers. . . .
Thou didst set a bound which they should not pass, so that they might not again cover the earth. . . .
When thou sendest forth thy Spirit, they are created; and thou renewest the face of the ground.

The Feast of Tabernacles, the third pilgrim festival, is sometimes referred to in Scripture as *the* feast (Ezek. 45:25) and also as the feast of the Lord (Judg. 21:19).

We may assume that this was the feast on which Elkanah, the father of Samuel, came to the sanctuary at Shiloh each year. At this feast, too, events are dramatized. People live in shelters open to the sky as a tangible reminder of the time when they lived in tents during the wilderness journey. This account, no doubt, is an explanation of a later date. The booths were already in use as part of the harvest festival and, furthermore, Israel did not live in booths but in tents during the wilderness journey. The festival itself is probably of Canaanite origin. In Judges 9:27 it is reported that the Canaanites of Shechem held a feast after the grape harvest in the temple of their god Baal. At the end of the book of Judges it is clear that the Feast of Tabernacles had been incorporated in the life of Israel. "Behold, there is the yearly feast of the LORD at Shiloh" (Judg. 21:19ff.). Hence, Israel gave to this agrarian festival a salvation-historical interpretation. The whole process was facilitated by the fact that the word *sukkot* can be translated by "tents" as well as "booths," which made possible the connection with the wilderness journey.

It is a feast with a universal eschatological perspective, for there will come a day, says Zechariah, on which "everyone that survives of all the nations that have come against Jerusalem shall go up year after year to worship" the Lord at the Feast of Booths (Zech. 14:16). It is an exuberant harvest festival at which there was dancing in the forecourt of the temple and of which it was said: "He who has not seen the rejoicing of this nocturnal festival has never seen rejoicing in his life."[49]

It was at the Feast of Tabernacles that the dedication of Solomon's temple was remembered (1 Kings 8:65), a feature that later disappeared. Upon the people's return from exile the feast acquired a new impulse. From Nehemiah we learn that in the seventh month Ezra the priest was requested to bring out "the book of the law of Moses" and to read from it (Neh. 8). In the course of the reading they came upon the passage in Leviticus 23:34-43, in which the command to celebrate the Feast of Tabernacles is given; and they promptly tore branches from the trees — from the olive tree, the wild olive, myrtle, palm, and other leafy trees — to make booths for themselves and to live in them for the duration of the feast. It is said that from the days of Joshua the Israelites had not done such a thing. The newness of it all can hardly refer to the booths themselves, for, considering the name of the feast, the booths were well known. The newness probably relates to the fact that the booths were now constructed in Jerusalem and specifically in the forecourt of the temple.

After the Exile Jerusalem became the center of the cult and the erection of booths in the forecourt was perhaps an expression of relocation. There was great rejoicing. "And day by day, from the first day to the last, he read from the book of the

49. Ibid., p. 447.

law of God. . . . They kept the feast seven days. . . ." (One cannot help asking if this is how the past of Simchat Torah — the Rejoicing with the Torah — began. In a later period it was celebrated in direct association with the Feast of Tabernacles.) In Nehemiah 8 we find no trace of "the fruit of goodly trees" to which there is reference in Leviticus 23:40. This is obviously a later development at which worshippers carried the fragrant *etrog* (a lemon-like fruit) in one hand and the *lulab* (a bundle of branches including palm, myrtle, and willow branches) in the other.

In the period of the prophets the feast was even more exuberant. On the night before the festival, to the accompaniment of flutes and the singing of songs, the crowds went up in procession to the mountain of the Lord, to the "Rock of Israel" (Isa. 30:29). Amos, who observed the feast as it was held in Bethel where it had become an occasion for drinking and revelry, pronounced judgment on it.[50] "I hate, I despise your feasts, and I take no delight in your solemn assemblies. . . . Take away from me the noise of your songs; to the melody of your harps I will not listen" (Amos 5:21ff.).

Amos illustrates the hard struggle that Israel had to wage to hold its own against Canaanite culture. The forms and conventions of this culture — it was the environment in which Israel breathed every day! — had to be structured and reinterpreted from within Israel's experiences with the saving action of God. During and after the captivity this process accelerated. The elements that make the feast a feast of nature — the agrarian motifs — recede into the background. The historicizing of the nature festivals continued. The centralization of the cult in Jerusalem caused the feasts to develop into pilgrim festivals. This was especially true of the Feast of Tabernacles because earlier in the year, during Passover and the Feast of Weeks, the peasants could hardly leave their work behind. Especially in the period of the Exile, and as a result of the identity crisis the

50. Hayyim Schauss, *The Jewish Festivals: History and Observance* (New York: Schocken Books, 1962), pp. 173f.

Exile forced upon Israel, the agrarian motifs receded. The historical and national aspects, such as the Exodus and the wilderness journey, began to dominate. In the period of the second temple the Passover gains in importance, but the Feast of Tabernacles remains of all feasts the most exuberant.

About the manner of observing the feasts in this period, a period in which Jesus' ministry took place as well, quite a lot is known.[51] People came as pilgrims from all parts of the land, as well as from the Diaspora, to celebrate the feast. On their way they sang the songs of ascent, the pilgrim songs (Pss. 120–134). Zion and Jerusalem are at the heart of these psalms. The community is central.

As for the celebration in the temple, the libation of water, the processions around the altar, and the torchlight procession are all striking ceremonies. On the morning of the first day of the feast a priest brought water from the fountain of Siloam in a golden flask. Upon his return, with the flask being carried at the head of the procession, there was the sound of trumpets at the Water Gate. Priests sang the words of Isaiah: "With joy you will draw water from the wells of salvation" (12:3). Next, the water was poured out into the basin near the altar. Again, the trumpets sounded and the people moved in procession, with *lulab* and *etrog*, around the altar. The Levites sang songs of praise, and when they recited the words, "Save us, we beseech thee, O LORD! O LORD, we beseech thee, give us success!" (Ps. 118:25), the crowds waved the *lulab* in unison and repeated the words. In the evening the ceremony of light was held in the forecourt, in the center of which the golden candlesticks burned. The worshippers, singing antiphonally, carried torches and danced.

In John's account of Jesus' public ministry the Feast of Tabernacles plays a significant role. In fact, his entire Gospel is structured in accordance with the Jewish liturgical calendar. Thrice there is mention of the celebration of Passover and once of the Feast of Tabernacles. The first reference to the Passover

51. Ibid., esp. pp. 180ff.

feast is made (2:13) in connection with the wedding at Cana (wine); the second follows the feeding of the five thousand in chapter 6 (bread). The following chapters (7–9) tell of events that took place during the Feast of Tabernacles and are sometimes called "The Narrative of the Feast of Tabernacles." Hanukkah, the feast of the rededication of the temple, forms the background of chapter 10. After chapter 11, which relates the raising of Lazarus (an image of the Resurrection), comes the third Passover celebration (chap. 12). This is the all-important one in which Jesus himself is the Passover lamb.

In chapters 7–9 Jesus links up with the symbolism of the Feast of Tabernacles. "On the last day of the feast, the great day, Jesus stood up and proclaimed, 'If any one thirst, let him come to me and drink. He who believes in me, as the scripture has said, "Out of his heart shall flow rivers of living water"'" (7:37-38). We must bear in mind that the water poured out in the temple stood for the water of the Torah that would water and make fruitful the whole earth.[52] In association with the illumination of the temple by the torchlight procession and candles Jesus said: "I am the light of the world; he who follows me will not walk in darkness, but will have the light of life" (8:12).

The booths in which Israel lived during the feast not only refer to the wilderness journey that occurred under God's protection; they also anticipate the "eternal tabernacles," the messianic time when God will dwell ("tabernacle") among people. It is an image the prophets used to depict the life of the righteous in the messianic kingdom. "My people will abide in a peaceful habitation, in secure dwellings, and in quiet resting places" (Isa. 32:18).

We also encounter the eschatological perspective of this feast in the New Testament: "Behold, the dwelling of God is with men. He will dwell with them, and they shall be his people" (Rev. 21:3). The background to this is found in Leviticus

---

52. P. A. Elderenbosch, *Het onderricht van de Messias* (Den Haag: Boekencentrum, 1976), p. 73.

26:11-12: "And I will make my abode ["tabernacle"] among you, and my soul shall not abhor you. And I will walk among you, and will be your God, and you shall be my people." In Zechariah 14:16 this promise is extended to all nations. The way in which this eschatological perspective is related to the Messiah comes out clearly in the story of the Transfiguration (Matt. 17:1-13). When the Torah and the Prophets (Moses and Elijah) appear and Jesus is transfigured, Peter thinks the end time has dawned and wants to erect tents for all three. But he is "jumping the gun." The transfiguration on the mountain is a reference to and an image of future glory.[53]

53. R. Boon, in *Mededelingen*, p. 66.

2. The Bible in the Liturgy

1. To Remember Is to Interpret

If in this chapter we attempt to answer the question how in various traditions the Bible began to function as a liturgical book, it is important that we first stop to consider the principles of biblical interpretation. How can we best do justice to the Bible as a liturgical book? To remember, after all, always entails the interpretation of what is on the liturgical agenda. In giving shape to remembrance one must be clear as to the interpretative contexts that must be taken into account.

In the previous chapter one of the most important viewpoints was already dealt with, namely the relationship between the Old and the New Testaments. The Old and the New Testaments constitute a unity and testify equally to the one revelation. The question is, What is the nature of that unity and how must it be handled? It has become ever clearer that underlying the shape of the Old Testament as we now have it is a certain idea or theme. The view of the final redactor was decisive: *that* is how at that time the Scriptures were understood. This does not mean, when we consider how the Scriptures function in the church, that the historical and literary studies of the Bible are now superfluous, but it does mean that they are subordinate to that central theme. Well, what is it? M. A. Beek has stated that in the course of his study he has increasingly begun to view the Old Testament as an Easter story.

"One can sense the preludes in the history of the patriarchs; after that the exodus from Egypt becomes the all-dominating event. Not only is it re-enacted and experienced in memorial every spring at Passover but, according to the commentator in Deuteronomy 5:15, it underlies every sabbath." "History is a series of repetitions of alternating slavery and deliverance up to and including the return from Babylonian captivity — and so it will be to the . . . end." "History was built around this theme, the prophets interpreted it, and the psalmists sang of it."[1] This thematic complex is further developed when the relationship between creation and redemption and, by extension, that between creation and the consummation, comes into view. In the Old Testament, the act of creation is an act of liberation, not so much a creation ex nihilo, or an explanation of the origin of the world. Creation and redemption are interwoven, as in the Psalms (Ps. 74:12-17; 89:5-13). In principle the creation story implicitly tells us "what God is like, as he made himself known in Israel and hence also in Jesus Christ."[2]

In the New Testament this line of thought is continued. There too, redemption, the Easter story, the resurrection, is the central theme. It was in the light of Easter that structures of observance developed in the early church. Sunday is the day of the resurrection. The New Testament, we may say, is an interpretation of the Old Testament in terms of faith in Jesus, the Messiah who fulfils the Scriptures. Rabbinical or Pharisaic Judaism is also an interpretation of the Old Testament (or Tanak), just as the interpretation of Sadducees was one that disappeared after the destruction of the temple in A.D. 70.

1. M. A. Beek, "Wijkende wegen," in M. A. Beek et al., *Spelregels* (Amsterdam: Polak en Van Gennep, 1967).
2. E. J. Beker and K. A. Deurloo, *Het begin in ons midden* (Baarn: Ten Have, 1977).

It is of some importance here to observe that the method of interpreting Scripture (the hermeneutics) employed by early Christians is no different from that of the rabbis.[3] For that reason, knowledge of rabbinical exegesis is indispensable to the interpretation of the Bible. For example, the manner in which Jesus in the Gospels interprets the Old Testament ties in with rabbinical exegesis. Jesus, as a Jewish rabbi, preached a radical doctrine that "contains unique renewals but as a whole maintains continuity with 'the oral Torah' which the Pharisees, by way of the elders and the prophets, received from Moses on Mt. Sinai."[4] Similarly, the preaching of the apostles, as it has been handed down to us in the book of Acts and in the apostolic letters (e.g., Hebrews), is an interpretation of the Old Testament. We are dealing here with processes of reinterpretation that got started after the captivity in Babylon, long before Jesus appeared on the scene, but that demand continuation. For that matter, this process of reinterpretation can be found already inside the Old Testament. Examples are the royal psalms, which are given a messianic interpretation after the Exile. This process is bound up with the nature of prophecy, which is not something to be interpreted in terms of the scheme of prediction and "coming true" but as fulfilment, a process that does not cease. Ever anew, prophecy as a divine and trustworthy utterance can enter a new phase of fulfilment (cf. pp. 13-15; also pp. 53, 55).

2. The Typological Structure

The manner in which the New Testament interprets the Old — the exegetical method followed by the early Christians — can be described as typological and was inseparable from the manner in which the early church dealt with the Bible liturgically.

---

3. A. Vis, *An Inquiry into the Rise of Christianity out of Judaism* (quoted by Beek; see p. 48 n. 1 above).

4. P. J. Tomson, "Gaaf zul je zijn zoals je hemelse Vader gaaf is," in *Geliefd is de mens* (Neukirchen-Vluyn: Neukirchener Verlag, 1981).

In a lengthy process of liturgical interaction with Scripture in the temple, the synagogue, and the early church, a complex of cross-connections (including reinterpretations) emerged with a high degree of internal cohesion. It forms the basis of rabbinical and early Christian exegesis. In virtue of this coherence one passage or pericope needs to be heard and explained in relation to other pericopes. The place in the context, the harmony between the parts, is fundamental.

In the typological approach Scripture is compared with Scripture and the deeper connections are tracked down. Often, unfortunately, the typological approach is falsely confused with the allegorical because the latter compares Scripture with the deposit of faith the church possesses (the creeds) and in terms of this possession searches for the deeper meaning and parabolic character of the biblical narratives. In typological exegesis, on the other hand, the search is aimed at discovering coherences within the Bible; it is a method given with Scripture itself.[5] For centuries, among the church fathers and elsewhere, this was the authoritative method of exposition. The rise of modern science, with its historical and literary analysis, has tended to discredit this approach. The result has been that a grasp of the coherence of the whole fell outside the field of vision of those who studied Scripture. Not that literary and historical approaches are without value; on the contrary. But they only have their place and meaning as aids to understanding the whole as it functioned in the community of faith. The search for a text behind the text, in the words of K. H. Miskotte, is "a cause without promise" for the interpretation of Scripture.

In this typological structure the biblical notion of time plays a fundamental role. In the last chapter (sec. 3) we already saw how important that concept of time is in the context of remembering, of celebrating the acts of God. Typological exegesis and liturgical celebration presuppose each other. The various units of time that occur in the Bible and that are expe-

5. J. M. Gerritsen, *Schepping, verlossing, voleinding: De verklaring van de heilige schrift* (Nijkerk: Callenbach, 1967), chap. 1.

rienced as a succession of events, like the day (the sun rises, the sun goes down), the month (from new moon to new moon), the year (seasons come, go, and return; the Hebrew word for "year" means repetition), human life (the son takes the place of the father; the word for "generation" suggests "a cycle of time") — all these time units have in common repetition, a cyclical movement. "What has been is what will be" (Eccl. 1:9).

The largest unit of time in the Bible, one of great importance for a good understanding of the relationship between the Old Testament and the New, is the *olam* (or "aeon" in the Greek). It is a period of duration that encompasses generations but that certainly may not be translated "eternity." It refers to a period so enduring that whatever belongs to the *olam* represents the things that endure. But even the *olam* ultimately repeats itself, and so one can speak of *olam* in the plural (*olamim*). God transcends all this, for he is from *olam* to *olam*, from everlasting to everlasting, as Psalm 90:2 puts it. God's kingship endures for all *olamim*, as Psalm 145:13 says, and the RSV translates this by "everlasting" (parallel with "all generations"). But, as was said above, the *olam* is also cyclical and ends when its circular course is completed. Then the *olam* is full, or fulfilled. As a result of God's action there is such a thing as history, progress or movement toward a consummation, a future.

After the Exile the idea arose that with the dawning of a new *olam* the Messiah would come. Christ, therefore, stands at the boundary between two *olamim*. Accordingly, John the Baptist could say, "the time is fulfilled, and the kingdom of God is at hand" (Mark 1:15). The followers of the Messiah will have a part in the new *olam* (Luke 20:35). The Old and New Testaments relate to two different *olamim*, even though God remains the same. In him the *olamim* are linked. In both periods one can speak of God's entering into time. God's dwelling with people in tabernacle and temple is associated with, can be called typical for, the incarnation in the new *olam*, with which the New Testament deals. Parenthetically, according to Scripture the ordering of the times is founded in the covenant with God. There is mention of the covenant of day and night (Jer. 33:20,

25) and the covenant that embraces succeeding generations (Gen. 17:9-10).

True, Israel broke that covenant, but God will renew it (Jer. 30 and 31). The letter to the Hebrews refers to the original covenant with Israel and its renewal accomplished by Christ. Jesus' statement, "This is my blood of the covenant" (cf. Matt. 26:28, RSV mg.), links up with the covenant of Sinai where it was said, "Behold the blood of the covenant which the Lord has made with you" (Ex. 24:8). Again, the covenant of Sinai is linked with the Abrahamic covenant.

We used the word "type" or "typical," and now we must discuss it further. Paul uses the word when in Romans (5:14) he calls Adam "a type of the one who was to come." In the past the word "foreshadowing" was often used, but that term fails to convey what is at stake. The reference is to Adam as archetype of Christ. To understand Christ one must first have seen Adam. The archetype visible in Adam is determinative. The stories of the Exodus and the wilderness journey are similarly to be understood as types for believers. In our discussion of the Feast of Tabernacles we already encountered the wilderness journey and living in tents as archetypes of the life of believers on their pilgrimage.

The sea, the cloud, the rock, the manna — all of these are archetypes in the New Testament of the way the sacraments mediate salvation. An archetype is also an example. According to Peter the presbyters must be examples (types) to the flock (1 Pet. 5:13). Of great importance is the typological significance of the tabernacle (and the temple), which in turn was made in accordance with the original model or type God had shown to Moses (Ex. 25:40). This fact is used in the letter to the Hebrews to make plain the intent of the life, death, and resurrection of Christ. Just as the tabernacle was made after the pattern shown by God to Moses and hence refers to God's invisible reality, so Christ is the image of the invisible reality of salvation that God has prepared. In the tabernacle God gave to people the means to approach and to meet him.[6] The same thing applies to the

6. R. Boon, *Op zoek naar de identiteit van de kerk* (Nijkerk: Callenbach, 1970), chap. 4.

revelation in Jesus Christ, an analogy that suggests the relationship between Jesus and the tabernacle. In sum, one can say that a typological connection exists between A and B when B is the fulfilment of A.[7] To fulfil, we must remember, is "to restore again," "to cause to answer to the original intention of a thing," "to make possible," "to fill full" in the sense of filling time with a specific content.

A question often raised (and answered in the affirmative) is whether this typological thought is antiquated. In place of this typological-symbolic kind of thought, after all, we have modern historical consciousness. Does that not mean that we must hold to the literal meaning of the text, as in the early church the Antiochene school already maintained over against the Alexandrian school?

Nevertheless, for centuries this typological structure formed the backbone of exegesis. Unfortunately, in Protestantism sensitivity to typological structures was lost at an early stage, a process linked with a strong dulling of liturgical consciousness.

N. Lohfink tried to find an answer to this question by proceeding from the story of the Exodus, which has been a typological feature in the liturgy of the Easter Vigil since the beginning of the church. In the *Exsultet*, the hymn sung to welcome the light of the Easter candle, the assumption is that the night of Easter and the night of the Exodus are the same. "The night in which once you led our fathers, the children of Israel, out of Egypt and guided them dry shod through the Red Sea," the night "in which Christ broke the bands of death and rose victoriously from the grave and the present night . . . in which those who repent are reconciled" — "all these nights are one and the same truly blessed night."[8] Embodied in this hymn is the essence of typological exegesis. "The gap in time no longer exists, the types coalesce, and the unity of the divine work of salvation is present in the act of worship." The question

---

7. Gerritsen, *Schepping, verlossing, voleinding*, p. 30.
8. N. Lohfink, *The Christian Meaning of the Old Testament* (Milwaukee: Bruce Publishing, 1968), pp. 67-86, esp. p. 70.

is whether within the framework of modern exegesis, whose concern is for the literal sense, this linkage can be maintained. If it cannot be shown, says Lohfink, that the biblical text is itself already "typological in its purpose," then we shall have to abandon this typology.

Then the reading of Exodus 14 and the *Exsultet* will have to disappear from the Easter liturgy. However, consider Exodus 15, a song in which the events of chapter 14 are celebrated as a hymn undoubtedly sung regularly in the liturgy of Israel. The song is among the most ancient texts of the Bible and is older, in any case, than chapter 14. It is not so much an account of historical events as a faith interpretation of them. In any event, the hymn concerns events that cannot be reconstructed by historical research. For example, "Thou didst stretch out thy right hand, the earth swallowed them" (v. 12), "Terror and dread fall upon them; because of the greatness of thy arm, they are as still as a stone, till thy people, O LORD, pass by" (v. 16). The song ends with the prospect of entry into the Promised Land, an event that will cause the nations to tremble. The remarkable thing here is that Israel's passage through the sea, as described in chapter 14, is absent. Central is a simple pattern of imagery: "There is a narrow passage, dangers threaten on the right and the left in the form of congealed masses of water, and men attempt to pass, rapidly and compelled by their inner desire, through the dangers to the other side of the danger zone."[9] This occurs in the verses 8–10:

> The deeps congealed in the heart of the sea. The enemy said, 'I will pursue, I will overtake, I will divide the spoil, my desire shall have its fill of them. I will draw my sword, my hand shall destroy them. Thou didst blow with thy wind, the sea covered them.

Thus the structure of the imagery is that of "passage through dangers threatening."[10] This structure recurs in the

9. Ibid., p. 82.
10. Ibid.

verses 12–17, where we are told how God led Israel into the Promised Land. Israel enters the land while the nations, struck still by the terror of Yahweh, stand by, unable to hold Israel back. Again we have the pattern of "a passage through dangers threatening." The threatening masses of the nations correspond here to the masses of water in the Sea of Reeds. "Just as God congeals the masses of water, so he now turns the nations to stone so that Israel can pass between them."[11]

Hence we find a typological structure within the song: passage through the Sea of Reeds is an archetype for the passage between the nations, now "turned to stone." In the same way the passage through the Red Sea can become an image for Christ's passage through death to his resurrection and hence for one's burial with Christ and resurrection to life as this is represented in baptism. The structure of the hymn of Exodus 15 is open to a number of typological applications.

Other examples are the Psalms — open structures which for that reason can play a central role in the Christian liturgy. Since Scripture itself contains typology (something very different from the allegorical exegesis some people in the early church practiced), there is no question of doing violence to modern consciousness by a typological explanation. G. von Rad, in his *Theology of the Old Testament*, came to similar conclusions on the basis of his discovery that within the Old Testament a process of continuing reinterpretation takes place. It means also that the fulfilment of prophecy never ends. Over and over a given prophecy can enter a new phase of fulfilment. When in the New Testament the images of the Old Testament are applied to Christ, in a sense the line of reinterpretation is continued.

For exegesis these are essential issues. De Knijff, who refers to the historical-metaphorical sense of the biblical stories, describes the core of the typological method in terms of a recognition of the biblical words and narratives as "bearers of

11. Ibid., p. 83.

the reality of divine action."[12] Every word in the Bible is a tone that is part of a melody and can therefore only be understood within the context of the whole.

Now that we have explained somewhat the principles of biblical exegesis as these were handled in past biblical Judaism and early Christianity, we return to the question of how the Bible as a liturgical book functioned in a number of traditions. Again, we can only offer an outline.

3. The Postbiblical Synagogal Tradition

That which has always been and still is characteristic for Jewish worship comes to expression in the Jewish word for liturgy: *awoda*. This word means not only liturgy but also labor. It implies that all of life is liturgy — service to God. The rules of liturgy and the rules of ethics have always formed a single whole. Saying the prayers is just as necessary as acting correctly toward one's neighbor. This unity comes to expression in the *halakah*, the total body of laws, ordinances, and legal decisions that shape the Jewish way of life. Despite the multicolored development of postbiblical Judaism, its continuity with the past remained very strong, stronger, that is, than in Christianity. Its liturgical formulations, arising in a process lasting many centuries but rooted in the biblical tradition, are in all but a few details the same the world over.

Initially, the liturgical life of Israel moved simultaneously in the channels of temple and synagogue. Historically, this parallel existence of the two came to an end in A.D. 70 when Jerusalem and the temple were destroyed. As far as we know, there were no tensions between the two institutions. We have some reason to think that priests served both in the temple and in the synagogue.[13]

Central in the temple services were the daily sacrifices,

12. H. W. de Knijff, *Sleutel en slot* (Kampen: Kok, 1980), pp. 35ff.
13. H. Mulder, *De synagoge in de niewtestamentische tijd*, Verkenning en bezinning (Kampen: Kok, 1969), p. 10.

the offerings of morning, midday, and evening; and of course
the temple was the center for the pilgrim feasts. Central in the
meetings of the synagogue was instruction in the Torah. After
the destruction of the temple, in the place of the daily sacrifices, came the prayers of morning, midday, and evening
(prayers, too, are sacrifices). The morning prayer was the most
important.[14] The heart of the daily prayers is the so-called
Amidah, which was prayed standing up and consisted of
nineteen (originally eighteen) benedictions. Preceding the
Amidah in the morning and the evening is the Shema, Israel's
creed: "Hear, O Israel: The LORD our God is one" (Deut. 6:4-9).
The complete Shema consists of these Scripture passages:
Deuteronomy 6:4-9, Deuteronomy 11:13-21, and Numbers
15:37-41. Preceding the Shema in the morning is a benediction
to praise God for the creation of light and in the evening
for the institution of day and night. The daily prayers were
ended with Alenu, which gives expression to the messianic
expectation concerning the coming of God's kingdom in this
world.

> Therefore we look to you, Lord our God, speedily to
> see the glory of your might, when the abominations will be
> removed from the earth. . . .
> Before you, Lord our God, may they bow and prostrate
> themselves, and to your glorious name give honor. May they
> all accept the yoke of your kingdom,/And rule over them
> speedily forever and ever,/For the kingdom is yours/And
> to all eternity you will reign in glory,/As is written in your
> Torah: "The Lord shall reign forever and ever."

Some scholars say that this prayer dates back seventeen
centuries.[15]
For the chanting of the daily prayers it is necessary to

14. For an extensive description, cf. H. H. Donin, *To Pray as a Jew:
A Guide to the Prayer Book and the Synagogue Service* (New York: Basic Books,
1980), chap. 3.
15. Bernard Martin, *Prayer in Judaism* (New York: Basic Books, 1968),
p. 143.

form a group of at least ten males above the age of thirteen, a so-called *minyan,* in order to lay stress upon the communal character of the Jewish service. Parts of the prayers can be prayed by the individual. But the prayers in which the name of God is sanctified may only be prayed by the group, for only in the presence of fellow Jews can one testify to God's holiness. This is true, for instance, in the Kaddish with which the morning prayer is concluded.

The Kaddish

Magnified and sanctified
Be God's great name
In the world he has created
According to his will.
May he establish his kingdom
During your lifetime and days
And during the lifetime
Of the whole house of Israel
Speedily and soon;
And say: amen.
May his great name be blessed
Forever and to all eternity.

Blessed and praised,
Glorified and exalted,
Extolled and honored
Magnified and lauded
Be the name of the Holy One, blessed be he,
Though he is high above
All the blessings and hymns,
Praises and consolations
That are spoken in the world;
And say: amen.

May there be great peace from heaven
And life for us and all Israel;
And say: amen.

May he who makes peace in his high places
Make peace for us and all Israel;
And say: amen.[16]

The Kaddish is very old, presumably predating the destruction of the temple. Certain phrases show a strong resemblance with the Lord's Prayer. It occupies an important place
in synagogal prayer. Every synagogue service can also be called
a prayer service. Prayers have a large place in it and the Jewish
Book of Prayers, the Siddur, is comprehensive.

It is well that we say a bit more here about the nature of
prayer as it occurs in the Jewish tradition. In various Christian
traditions the practice of prayer has become quite impoverished;
reorientation and deepening are urgently needed.

A fundamental datum is that prayer does not arise from
human desire but from God's desire.[17] It is God's will that
humans pray. Or, as tradition formulates it, it is an ordinance
to pray every day, for it has been said: "You shall serve the
LORD your God" (Ex. 23:25). That is, you shall serve him with
all your heart, says Deuteronomy (11:13), and, according to the
wise, that means prayer. Prayer is laid upon believers by a
command, a command involving both obligation and privilege.
If we had not first been addressed by God, we would not be
able to speak to him. This leads one to the conclusion that at
bottom prayer is not a question but an answer (Van Uden).

Abraham Heschel, the Jewish philosopher, distinguishes
two main types of prayer: the *expressive*, giving utterance to
feelings (of sorrow, joy, anxiety, etc.), and the *empathic,* the sense
of "feeling our way into" that arises when we use the words
of a formulated prayer.[18] Not expressive but empathic prayer
is the most common. For this last-mentioned form of prayer

16. Ibid., p. 147.
17. For an overview of prayer in the Jewish tradition, cf. H. H.
Donin, *To Pray as a Jew.*
18. A. J. Heschel, *Man's Quest for God: Studies in Prayer and Symbolism*
(New York: Charles Scribner's Sons, 1954), pp. 28ff.

one does not have to be in the proper mood. "Through the imaginative projection of our consciousness into the meaning of the words and through empathy for the ideas with which the words are pregnant, this type of prayer comes to pass. The word comes first; the feeling follows."[19]

Now it appears that in the Bible expressive and spontaneous prayer is the most common. Think, for example, of the Psalms and the prayers of Moses, Hannah, Solomon, Hezekiah, Jonah, and Jesus. In the Bible we also encounter fixed prayers, such as the priestly benediction in Numbers (6:24-26), the prayers accompanying the offering of the firstfruits (Deut. 26:5-10) and of the tithes (Deut. 26:13-15), and the Lord's Prayer (Matt. 6:9-13). It is clear that, following the Exile, the fixed prayers became even more important. The most ancient formulations — say, of the Eighteen Benedictions — stem, it is believed, from no later than the second century B.C. In this line of thought lies the request of Jesus' disciples for words with which to pray, just as John the Baptist taught his disciples (Luke 11:1). We must realize, however, that free prayer in the Bible only occurs in the case of a few prominent persons. The formulation of prayers as it increasingly took place after the Exile must be viewed as an effort to teach the people to pray. Prayer now falls within the reach of everyone.

The disparagement of formulated prayer as this sometimes comes to expression in Christian circles has no basis in the Bible and tradition but is a product rather of modern subjectivism and individualism. Says Heschel: it is more inspiring to let the heart echo the music of the ages than to play upon the broken flutes of our own hearts. "It is good that there are words sanctified by ages of worship, by the honesty and love of generations."

Add to this that prayer is not only something that we do — in prayer something also happens to us. Only by degrees do we begin to realize the meaning of the words; gradually we rise to the heights of prayer and find release from our daily

19. Ibid., p. 28.

cares. The words of a prayer, says Heschel, are like an island in the world. Every time we approach it the island must be conquered anew. Slowly we plod forward, through depths and heights, by side roads and detours, from word to word. "Arriving, we discover a level where words are treasures, where meanings lie hidden still to be mined."[20]

Another important dimension of the formulated prayer is that the words are directed not only to God but also to ourselves. Prayer to God is at the same time an assignment to the one who prays. To thank God for food at the same time means to see to it that one's fellow human has something to eat. To pray "Thy kingdom come" also implies the mandate to work at that kingdom. We address words to God; but the words turn around to address us. Hence, prayer is dialogic in structure. The Hebrew word for prayer, says Lionel Blue, can also be translated by "to work on oneself."[21]

"A Jew prays so that he can work on himself for the sake of God and shift his own will to become a better instrument of God's will." God does not need our prayers. Says an old proverb: "Prayer exists for man; righteousness exists for God." God does need humans; with them he made a covenant. For that reason people need to be forever reminded of their obligations. That is the reason for prayer. The relationship between God and man is one of reciprocity. God blesses humans, but in the benedictions (*berakot*) humans bless God. This is a biblical commandment. "You shall eat and be full, and you shall bless the LORD your God for the good land he has given you" (Deut. 8:10). In the Eighteen Benedictions the statement "Blessed be Thou, Lord our God, King of the Universe" occurs numerous times. God is blessed for everything, for nothing exists by itself. Jewish life is so structured that in all things the hidden love and wisdom of God are observed. In the synagogue prayers play such a large role that it can also be called the *beth ha-tefillah*, the house of prayer. To this must

20. Ibid., p. 29.
21. Lionel Blue, *To Heaven, with Scribes and Pharisees: The Jewish Path to God* (New York: Oxford University Press, 1976), p. 62.

immediately be added, however, that the same synagogue can also be called *beth ha-midrash,* or house of study. This brings us to our next point.

A second important part of the synagogue service, in addition to the prayers, is the public reading of the Torah and the reading of the prophets that goes with it. For this, too, a *minyan,* ten males over the age of thirteen, is needed. Just as in the beginning of the calendar, so today the reading is from a handwritten Torah scroll of parchment. The Torah has been divided into 54 sections, called Sedarim, so that the whole of it can be read from week to week in a year. On the morning of the sabbath a section, called a sidra or seder, is read. This sidra is then subdivided into seven *parashot,* followed by a fixed reading from the prophets, which usually has some connection with the sidra in question. At the readings it is customary to call to the front a number of persons whose task it is to pronounce a benediction before and after the sidra being read by the official reader. The reading from the prophets (the haftarah) is done by the person called forward. The latter custom is very old, and we already find it in the New Testament, when in the synagogue at Nazareth Jesus read the passage from Isaiah (Luke 4:16).

The sidra is not so much read aloud as chanted by the precentor or hazan. The precentor also sings the liturgical songs and the prayers.[22] The hazan, not the rabbi, leads the service. The task of the rabbi lies in the house of study.

The cycle of one year in which the entire Torah is read through is known as the Babylonian cycle. Initially, there also was a three-year Palestinian cycle. This, however, is no longer available for study in all its parts. There are indications that this cycle lasted three-and-a-half years and had no fixed connections between pericopes and seasons. Continuous reading probably began in the second century. Scholars have tried to reconstruct a three-year cycle, positing that at Passover the

22. For further information about the synagogue service, cf. Abraham Millgram, *Jewish Worship* (Philadelphia: Jewish Publication Society of America, 1971); Leo Trepp, *The Complete Book of Jewish Observance* (New York: Behrman House Inc./Summit Books, 1980).

stories of the Exodus (Ex. 12) and the Passover in the wilderness (Num. 9) were read. The third Passover reading was from Genesis 4 (the death of Abel). At Pentecost the stories of the Tower of Babel and the giving of the Torah on Mt. Sinai (Ex. 20) were read. Considerable problems arise, however, in connection with the great Day of Atonement. Then Leviticus 16 would have to be read, but this does not fit in with the reconstruction. Similar problems arise in connection with the Feast of Tabernacles. It could be that at the festivals the continuous reading was interrupted and therefore the cycle was detached from the festivals.

The associated readings from the prophets (the haftaroth) vary greatly in length. Presumably, the reason was that people wanted to end on a note of joy and kept on reading till they found one, if need be, in a following book of the Bible. Conv· ·sely, a haftarah can also be very small, as small as one verse. Later, after the Babylonian cycle had pushed aside the Palestinian, the minimum length to be read from the Torah was set at 21 verses. More than half of the Palestinian haftaroth were taken from Isaiah, specifically Deutero-Isaiah. The Babylonian haftaroth were largely borrowed from the Palestinian ones.

In the synagogue service the reading from the Torah was central. The prophets and writings were understood as explanations and applications of the Torah that set the theme. In considering the question of the connection between a sidra and a haftarah, one must realize that in rabbinical exegesis the verbal association is the determining category. Even words or groups of words are important points of contact. But this is not all. The typological structures all play a large role in rabbinical exegesis. We find an example of the rabbinical method in the New Testament where Paul (Gal. 4:27) applies Isaiah 54:1 to Genesis 21, a chapter that features Sarah. We encounter something similar in the Palestinian cycle where Isaiah 54 is selected as a haftarah on Genesis 16, with the words "she bore him no children" marking the connection.

An important point is that rabbinical exegesis — an exegesis strongly shaped by key words and themes — does not function so much in the context of preaching as in that of

THE BIBLE IN THE LITURGY

halakah or ethics. As a result, the ancient synagogue never developed a biblical theology.[23]

The Psalms occupy an important place in the Jewish liturgy. Half of the Psalms form part of the Siddur, the prayer book. In the morning prayer alone more than twenty psalms have been incorporated. Already earlier we encountered certain groupings of psalms: the Hallel at Passover and the Feast of Tabernacles (Pss. 113–118) and the pilgrim songs (Pss. 120–134). In addition there is also a relationship between the Torah readings and the Psalms, at least where the three-year cycle is concerned.[24]

The book of Psalms is divided into five parts that correspond to the five books of the Torah. In most Bible editions these five Psalm books are marked. The first volume, Psalms 1-41, runs parallel with Genesis, though Psalm 1 relates more to the entire Torah than specifically to Genesis: "Blessed is the man" whose "delight is in the law of the LORD, and on his law he meditates day and night." The second volume, which opens with Psalm 42, links up with the beginning of Exodus, the oppression in Egypt. "I say to God, my rock: 'Why hast thou forgotten me? Why go I mourning because of the oppression of the enemy?'" (42:9). The third, beginning with Psalm 73, ties in with Leviticus. In Psalm 73 there is mention of a priest who gains insight when he enters the sanctuary of God (v. 17). The fourth volume, tying in with Numbers, starts with Psalm 90 where the theme is the insignificance of man, a kind of correction of the census described in Numbers 1 and 2. (A similar correction is added to the story of David's census in 1 Chronicles 21.) The fifth volume, beginning with Psalm 107, corresponds with Deuteronomy; its special psalm, Psalm 119, is itself divided into 22 strophes that tie in with the middle section of Deuteronomy (chaps. 4–28).

In the concluding chapter of Deuteronomy Moses is given a glimpse of the Promised Land. This in turn is echoed in Psalm

23. R. Zuurmond, "De drie-jaarlijkse cyclus van de Thora-lezingen," *Eredienst* 8 (1974): 91-128.
24. Cf. liturgical dictionaries, under Psalms.

64

150, the psalm of praise that completes the book of Psalms. The connections also appear when a person notices the relations with the feasts. In the first year, at the Passover, Genesis 3 and 4 are read, where mention is made of the firstfruits of orchard and flock. Psalm 4 exhibits the same motif: "Offer right sacrifices and put your trust in the LORD" (v. 5). Exodus 12, read in the second year, accords well with Psalm 52:1: "Why do you boast, O mighty man . . . against the godly?" The third Passover celebration, the first to be observed in the wilderness (Num. 9), is associated with Psalm 100: "Make a joyful noise to the LORD, all the lands!" Used in this manner the psalms are responses to the Sabbath readings, not on the part of the individual but of the entire worshipping community of Israel.

In conclusion, in this section concerning the postbiblical tradition of the synagogue, we must mention the development of the liturgical year as an important ordering principle in Israel's liturgical association with the Tanak. We have already discussed the readings from the Torah and the prophets and the place of the Psalms in that context. As far as the writings are concerned, five of them have been given a special place on the calendar of annual feasts. These are the so-called festive scrolls. At Passover the Song of Solomon is read; at the Feast of Weeks, the book of Ruth; on the ninth day of Ab (the day the destruction of the temple is commemorated), the Lamentations of Jeremiah; at the Feast of Tabernacles, Ecclesiastes; and at the Feast of Purim, the book of Esther. In the previous chapter we referred to the great pilgrim festivals, two of which occur in the spring of the year. In the postbiblical period especially the autumnal feasts have come into their own.

We shall now discuss the autumn festivals, restricting ourselves to the great festive month of Tishri. It begins with the Jewish New Year — Rosh Hashanah — followed by ten days of penitence, and concluding with the great Day of Atonement, Yom Kippur. The entire sequence is known as the Days of Awe.[25]

25. Cf. S. Y. Agnon, *Days of Awe*, 2nd ed. (New York: Schocken Books, 1965).

Tishri is the seventh month; it seems strange that New Year should fall on the first day of the seventh month. One would rather think the first month, Nisan, the month of the Exodus, would qualify for this honor. It seems that the linkage with Yom Kippur, the atmosphere of self-examination, reflection, and new beginning, is the deciding factor here.

Preceding Rosh Hashanah is the month Elul, a period of preparation for the Days of Awe. Every day the shofar is sounded as a call to penitence. The period from the first of Elul to the tenth of Tishri (Day of Atonement) is exactly forty days. According to tradition, the people performed acts of penitence in this period, in which Moses returned to the mountain to receive new tables of the law, and which ended when he came back with them on the tenth of Tishri. This period of forty days remained a penitential period ever after. The prayers of penitence begin already the week before Rosh Hashanah.

> Lo! as the potter mouldeth plastic clay
> To forms his varying fancy doth display;
> So in Thy hand, O God of love, are we;
> Thy hand regard, let sin be veil'd from Thee.

In the succeeding stanzas the metaphors of the mason, the smith, the seaman, and so on, replace that of the potter.[26]

There is fasting, and the mood of Teshuah, the return to God, possesses people. Rosh Hashanah is the Day of Judgment, the Day of Remembrance, the day of sounding the shofar. On this day it is sealed "who shall live and who shall die," depending on the deeds done as they are recorded in the Book of Life. According to legend, this book lies open on this day. According to tradition, Rosh Hashanah is also the birthday of creation; its emphasis is therefore on God's kingship over the world. The roots of this day can be found in Leviticus 23:23: "In the seventh month, on the first day of the month, you shall observe a day

---

26. L. Hirsch, *De wereld van het joodse geloof* (Baarn: Bosch en Keuning, 1964), p. 116. The English version is from A. Millgram, *Jewish Worship*, p. 250.

of solemn rest, a memorial proclaimed with blast of trumpets, a holy convocation." On this day people dress themselves in the white garments of death. Torah curtains, Torah mantles — all coverings are white.

In the morning prayer the so-called Avinu Malkenu is recited: "Our father, our king, we have sinned before you." On the first day (in the evening) the Torah reading concerns the birth of Isaac; on the second (the morning prayer) it deals with the sacrifice of Isaac. The haftarah with the first reading relates to the birth of Samuel. (Isaac and Samuel were two children in whose life the power of God was manifest.) The haftarah with the reading concerning the sacrifice of Isaac is Jeremiah 31:2-20, where the subject is Israel's return from exile and Rachel's weeping over her children. After the readings from the Torah the shofar is sounded — and that in a variety of ways. Reasons given for sounding the shofar are:[27]

1. Remembrance of God's rule over the world
2. Call to repentance
3. Call to listen to and obey the Torah
4. Remembrance of the warnings of the prophets
5. Remembrance of the storming of the walls of Jerusalem
6. Remembrance of Abraham's willingness to offer to God that which was dearest to him
7. The evocation of fear before God
8. The beginning of judgment and longing for the Messiah
9. Remembrance of the beginning of the Year of Jubilee: the beginning of new freedom
10. Remembrance of the resurrection of the dead.

The general idea is that the sounding of the shofar brings us to God's remembrance. The theme of Rosh Hoshanah is the connection between the creation of the world and the obligation of humans as the crown of creation so to arrange the world that

27. L. Hirsch, *De wereld*, pp. 119ff.

it answers to its original purpose. The service on this day is very long; its motifs are worked out in numerous variations. All the prayers (also those which are prayed daily) and all the readings are supported by a special melody and distinct rhythm — urgent, solemn, imploring. The prayers of the congregation alternate with those of the cantor. The returning refrains, like the liturgical chants, become ever more haunting and moving:

> The king grasps the ends of the earth,
> Shakes the evildoers from the earth,
> And a loud cry arises in heaven and on earth:
> How glorious is thy name on the whole earth!
> As he rules on earth
> the depths of the earth cry out,
> heaven shouts, and the earth rejoices.

The refrain reads: "Three times he sounds the trumpet on earth: all its inhabitants tremble."

On this day also the Alenu, which is said to date from the first centuries and is prayed daily at the end of every prayer service, has a distinct flavor. It begins with the words: "We rise to our duty to praise the Lord of all, to acclaim the Creator." At the words "we bend the knee and bow, proclaiming Him as King of kings," the entire congregation and the cantor bow down in adoration. Striking also is that in the prayers the sacrifice of Isaac becomes the ground for pleading with God: "Permit to appear before your eye the sacrifice when our father Abraham bound his son Isaac on the altar and restrained his compassion to do your will with his whole heart; in your goodness turn away your burning wrath from your people, from your city, and from your heritage."

Before the shofar is sounded, Psalm 47 is recited, not with exuberance but with restraint:

"God has gone up with a shout, the LORD with the sound of a trumpet. Sing, . . . sing praises to our King!"

Then three distinct shofar notes are called out by the rabbi and the shofar is sounded: first, a long-drawn-out sound, the *tekiah*, a call to reflection; next the *shevarim*, three short blasts;

then the *teruah*, a series of sharp staccato sounds; and in conclusion the *tekiah* again, as the call to awaken.

Following Rosh Hashanah, the days leading to Yom Kippur are days of inwardness in which observing Jews make an effort to restore broken relationships. In Judaism the restoration of one's relationship to a fellow human being is at least as important as the restoration of one's relationship with God. We can only count on forgiveness by God when we have made amends for our own mistakes. One author refers in this connection to the similarity with the first letter of John: "If any one says, 'I love God' and hates his brother, he is a liar" (1 John 4:20).[28]

It is a period of intense self-examination that not infrequently leads to confession of sin.

Then comes Yom Kippur. It is regarded as an extra sabbath, the Sabbath of sabbaths (Lev. 16:31). It is a twenty-four-hour fast and people stay in the synagogue throughout the day. On the evening before, the people sing the age-old and very moving Kol Nidré, the prayer with which Yom Kippur begins. In the strict sense it is not a prayer but a legal declaration, an Aramaic text more than a thousand years old with a Bible verse at the beginning and end. The contents are concerned with release from rashly assumed vows made to oneself. In the past the practice often led to misunderstandings, as though by this device Jews could free themselves from agreements they had made with others. But Kol Nidré has nothing to do with such a thing!

The melody is perhaps more important than the text, for it sounds like the voice of conscience, the lament arising from failure. In some synagogues the text has been replaced by Psalm 130, while the melody has been kept. According to Rabbi Soetendorp, Psalm 130 occupied a place in the Yom Kippur liturgy already in the period of the second temple.[29]

28. W. Zuidema, *God's Partner* (Baarn: Ten Have, 1977), p. 137.
29. J. Soetendorp, *Symboliek der joodse religie* (Hilversum: W. de Haan, 1966), p. 197.

69

The Kol Nidré concludes with Numbers 15:26: "And all the congregation of the people of Israel shall be forgiven, and the stranger who sojourns among them, because the whole population was involved in the error," a passage recited out loud by everyone.

On Yom Kippur morning, afternoon, and evening, prayer constitutes one whole, as it were. The service lasts, without interruption, the whole day until dark. Many confessions of sin are recited. During the Alenu prayer people kneel. In the morning Leviticus 16 is read from the Torah. This section deals with the service in the temple on the great Day of Atonement. Next to be read is Numbers 29:7-11, where the instructions for its observance are found. The accompanying haftarah is Isaiah 57:14–58:14, a passage in which there is comfort for the contrite, fasting for the sake of form is condemned, and people are called to live in conformity with the Torah. At the beginning of the afternoon prayer there is another reading from the Torah, this time from Leviticus 18, this one directed against unchastity and sacrificing children to Moloch. The associated haftarah is the entire book of Jonah — Jonah who could not elude his calling. Then there is the narrative concerning the high priest who was permitted to enter the innermost sanctuary only on this day and was only then allowed to pronounce the name of God, a name that otherwise might not be pronounced.

At the end of the service all recite the Shema, followed by, "Praised be His name whose glorious kingdom is for ever and ever." The shofar sounds once more and the service is over.

A celebration with such intensity, one has to acknowledge, is unknown to Christianity. Neither does the Christian liturgy have anything that parallels the profound and urgent character of these confessions of sin. This is something one can do only once a year. Given such intensity, weekly repetition is impossible; and as a Christian one has to ask whether a weekly confession of sin and proclamation of pardon does not lead to a hallowing out that is questionable indeed.

Five days after Yom Kippur comes Sukkoth, the Feast of Tabernacles discussed in the previous chapter. Little needs to

70

be added at his point. Again one is struck by the directness of people's experience with things. Everyone is personally involved. The booths have to be homemade; no carpenter may be hired to do the job! This is of inestimable importance for the transmission of the experience and insights of one generation to another. Now that there no longer is a temple or altar people form a procession with the lulab around the bima (the reader's table).

On the twenty-third day of Tishri the great month of festivals is concluded with Simchat Torah, "Rejoicing in the Law." This is the day the one-year cycle of Torah readings is completed. The last part of Deuteronomy is read — the chapter that tells of Moses' death after he had been permitted to cast a glance on the Promised Land. The person invited to perform this reading is called "the bridegroom of the Torah." Immediately after this a new start is made by reading the first verses of Genesis. The person called up for this is called *Hatan Bereshit* (the Bridegroom of Genesis). The spirit of the service is very joyful; the Torah scrolls are carried around the synagogue seven times in procession. In some areas worshippers dance with the scrolls; they sing the song of the Torah.

> I will exult and jubilantly rejoice with this Torah;
> it is our strength and light. . . .
> Abraham, Isaac, Jacob, Aaron, Joshua, Samuel,
> Solomon, Elijah, all rejoiced in the joy of Torah.
> Torah is the tree of life; it is life unto all,
> for with you is the fountain of life.

One day, says the tradition, the Messiah will return on Simchat Torah.

4. The Early Christian and Catholic Tradition

Since the early Christian churches were Jewish, we may assume that the manner in which the Scriptures functioned liturgically reflected to some degree the liturgy of the synagogue. We know from the book of Acts that the early Christians also went to the temple and observed the hours of prayer. The Old Testament was their Bible.

What was new was the breaking of bread in homes (Acts 2:46) — the celebration of communion — and the celebration of baptism. From the very beginning Word and sacrament are the marks of the Christian liturgy. We find this fundamental structure very clearly, in Luke's Gospel, in the story of the disciples going to Emmaus (Luke 24). In this story we read of the opening of the scriptures and the breaking of bread.[30]

The facts regarding the celebration of the New Testament church can be summarized as follows. Believers met in homes, especially on the first day of the week, the day of Resurrection. They ate a meal together, read the scriptures, sang psalms and hymns, sometimes responsively. It is almost as if the prayers, the hymns, and the confessions ran together and fused. People explained the scriptures, preached, prophesied, spoke in tongues. The Lord's Supper or the Eucharist was celebrated with great joy as a salvation meal with the risen Lord. At this time the mighty acts of God were remembered and experienced anew. Believers shared the food they brought. The whole event had a fluid, dynamic character.[31] In much of this the Jewish origins are evident. Jewish Christian influence, manifest in the observance of the law and the dating of Easter, must have been strong right into the fourth century. Believers appealed to the authority of James, "the brother of the Lord."[32]

The heart of the Christian worship service, derived as it was from the Jewish liturgy, was commemorative doxology. It can be described as praise-filled thanksgiving, thanksgiving in which the name of the Lord was invoked and the mighty acts

30. N. A. Schuman, *Een reisverhaal — leesoefeningen in Lucas* (Den Haag: Boekencentrum, 1981), pp. 165ff.
31. J. van der Werf, *Kleine liturgiek* (Den Haag: Boekencentrum, 1965).
32. These and the following data are mainly taken from H. A. J. Wegman, *Geschiedenis van de christelijke eredienst in het Westen en in het Osten* (Hilversum: Gooi en Sticht, 1976), pp. 21ff.

of creation and the covenant were acclaimed. In all this the attention of the worshippers was directed toward Jesus Christ as the Messiah and the risen Lord. This commemorative or anamnetic prayer is based on the experience of God's presence and his acts of redemption.

Important here is the thought — an idea also derived from the Jewish tradition — that the liturgy on earth reflects the glory of the heavenly liturgy and at the same time offers a perspective on the consummation of the world. This in turn is bound up with the notion that mankind reflects the glory of God (in a hidden, indirect way), for direct vision is still reserved for the future. In all this Jesus is the perfect image of God.

In addition to the weekly celebration of communion on Sunday the Christian church, from the second and third century on, had a daily prayer service with a fixed basic pattern that included psalms, hymns, and prayers. In the morning prayer the scriptures were read and explained. (In the last chapter [sec. 6] we already discussed the relationship between the Sabbath and Sunday.)

In the early years of the church Easter became the central feast, one already celebrated in the second century. In the New Testament we do not read of it as such, though the meaning of the Passover festival for Christians does come up (cf. 1 Cor. 5:6-8). The date of Easter occasioned much strife. In Asia Minor, Easter was initially observed on the date of the Passover festival, the 14th or 15th of Nisan, while in the West it was observed on the night of the first Saturday after that date. The emphasis in the first tradition lies on remembering the death of the Lord; in the Roman tradition, also followed in Palestine, the accent lies on Jesus' Resurrection.

Wegman, in his history of Christian worship, reconstructs the celebration of Easter as follows. During the night — the service was called the Easter Vigil — believers came together to hear from Scripture about the offering up of the Passover lamb, the sacrifice of Isaac, the suffering servant of Isaiah, and about the suffering and death of Jesus. This vigil was part of a period of fasting (lasting one or more days) and was concluded toward morning, at the hour of daybreak, with the celebration of communion. This also signified the end of the fast, the end of grieving over the death of Jesus; believers then began the joyous celebration of the fifty-day Easter season. The Eucharist was understood and experienced as participation in the life of the Lord as "an earnest of the Resurrection." The fiftieth day, the day of Pentecost, concluded the Easter season in which people prayed standing up as a symbol of the Resurrection, and in which there was no fasting. Thus Easter had a double focus: fasting on account of the death of the Lord (the bridegroom who had been taken away — Mark 2:20), a period (the vigil) in which Christ as the Passover Lamb who was slain was central, and the celebration of the Eucharist as the beginning of the joyful fifty-day period during which the people anticipated the swift return of the Lord.

Initially, there was no baptism during the Easter vigil. It was not until the third century that baptism as the rite of initiation into the mysteries of salvation and of incorporation into the church was given a fixed place. Baptism was not something incidental but a symbolic path of conversion. At first, people in certain occupations, such as the military, were excluded. After admission followed the catechumenate, a period in which catechumens were given instruction in Christian doctrine and ethics. In this period special prayer services for catechumens were held. Then followed a period, the so-called period of the *electi*— those who were found worthy to be baptized — which was a direct preparation for baptism, a period later to coincide with the time of fasting six weeks before Easter. Baptism, which was administered preferably during the Easter vigil, consisted of the renunciation of Satan and one's pagan past, of confessing one's faith before immersion, of the laying on of hands, and the anointing of head and body, the kiss of peace, and the celebration of communion together with the church. It is likely that most parts of the administration of baptism were of Jewish origin.

About the weekly worship service in the first period we

have a good deal of information from Justin Martyr (ca. A.D 138). Believers heard from the Old Testament a reading that was now in process of formation, though there was yet no established lectionary. An exposition followed. Then came the intercessions, concluded with the kiss of peace. Communion was next. The people themselves brought the bread and the wine. An improvised eucharistic prayer was said. Communion at this time was no longer a real meal as it initially had been. What did remain was the pronouncing of a blessing over the bread and wine, as was done at Jewish meals. The liturgical pattern of Scripture and table was fully present. In the ministry of the Word the Old Testament naturally occupied an important place because the preaching of Jesus and the apostles was based on the law and the prophets.

Not much is known about the period preceding this. We do know from the Didache—the teaching of the Twelve Apostles (ca. A.D. 100)—that at that time the Lord's Supper was still combined with the celebration of the love feast or agape.

A new liturgical period dawned when the Christian church was officially recognized in A.D. 313. From being clandestine, the church now was able to move to a centrally located basilica. The liturgy grew more elaborate. The typology expressing itself in the notion that the life of the church, including its worship, was a continuation of God's work of salvation, began to play a large role in Christian art. In the fourth and fifth centuries, we witness a large measure of creativity in the sphere of worship. We know about the liturgical life of Jerusalem, an important center of worship, from a travel journal kept by Egeria, a Spaniard who visited Jerusalem around A.D. 415.

From his account we learn that the daily morning prayer consisted of songs of praise and intercessions. A Scripture reading was added only on Sundays. The vespers had a fuller liturgy. They were called "lucernarium," because in this service the lamps were lit from the light that always burned in the grotto of the church of the Holy Sepulchre. Psalms 130–141 were of central significance (Ps. 141, we may note, was also part of the Jewish evening prayers.) In addition to Psalms, evening hymns were sung. Besides the liturgy of the hours there were services in which the Eucharist was celebrated. In these services the readings from Scripture and their interpretation became increasingly important. A certain order of pericopes developed for reading on Sundays and other festive days. The congregation still sang (responses and antiphones, for instance).

Whereas in an earlier period there was mention only of Sunday observance and the celebration of Easter, at this point a sort of church year begins to take shape. Mention is made of Epiphany, the feast of the baptism of Jesus, followed by a period of fasting lasting eight weeks and ending with the observance of Holy Week (Palm Sunday, Maundy Thursday, Good Friday, Holy Saturday, and Easter Vigil), Easter, Ascension, and Pentecost. This calendar of feast days was adopted both by the Eastern church and by the Western.

What is striking in this period is that in Jerusalem and other places as well the monks who initially lived alone as hermits now took part in the liturgy. Under their influence the Scripture readings gained a larger place in the worship services. Besides the Psalms, other parts of the Old and New Testaments were read. The congregation reacted with responses that developed into hymnic texts. The tenor of these responses is that in them the texts of the Old Testament were explained in the light of the New.

Both in the East and in the West an independent rite developed, in each of which a variety of local differentiations occurred. Wegman has pointed out that the meaning of the word "rite" must not be defined too narrowly.[33] Included in it is not merely the notion of an order of service but "the whole of a spiritual legacy" to which belong the liturgy, the spirituality, popular piety, the discipline, and the theology concealed in it. "One does not know an Eastern rite simply because one knows all about the external forms."

33. Ibid., p. 73.

4. The Early Christian and Catholic Tradition

In this period the West has, for example, a Roman, a Milanese, a Spanish (Visigothic), and a Gallican rite. In time the Roman (papal) rite was to overshadow all the others because developments in Jerusalem, as we noted earlier, exerted strong influence. In the Roman rite also, morning prayer and vespers were meant for the whole congregation, clergy as well as laity. If for some reason one was unable to attend these services, he was obligated to pray the Lord's Prayer and say the Apostles' Creed at home. The morning prayers consisted of Psalms 148–150 and probably Psalms 63 and 51, plus the canticles of Exodus 15, Deuteronomy 32, and Daniel 3. Psalms 141 and 142, plus the burning of incense, were central in the vesper service ("Let my prayer be counted as incense before thee," says Ps. 141:2, an action also familiar to the church of the New Testament, as is evident from Rev. 5:8.)

The fundamental structure of the daily liturgy of the hours is psalms, prayers, intercessions, and the Lord's Prayer, supplemented by hymnic and meditative texts. Examples available to us have the form of a litany (petitions) concluded with the Kyrie Eleison ("O Lord, have mercy"). It is clear, therefore, that the Jewish custom, to praise God both morning and evening as a congregation of the Lord, is still in vogue in the church of the fourth and the fifth centuries. In Rome, under monastic influence, the number of daily services increased thereafter. The result was that increasingly these services were of interest only to monastic communities and the clergy. In the West also, under the impact of the same influence, the canticles of the Old and the New Testament and the organized reading of Scripture were introduced. (In the East, one notes, there is less divergence in spirituality between the people and the clergy.) For the Sunday services a roster of Scripture readings, especially for the Easter cycle, began to circulate. Wednesdays and Fridays were and continue to be days of fasting; on these days, services of the Word were held in Rome.

Easter developed into the so-called Triduum, which embraced Good Friday, Holy Saturday, and Easter Sunday. To be precise, in accordance with the biblical division of the day, it

77

began at sundown on Maundy Thursday. As a result, what was initially observed as a unit — namely, the death and resurrection of Christ — was now spread over several days. The typology of the Passover lamb receded into the background, probably a result of the growing alienation between Jews and Christians. The idea of the Triduum is, as it were (as that was done in Jerusalem), to imitate the course of Jesus' life and to allegorize it — that is, to relate it to the course of the Christian life.

Starting here was a process in which the remembrance of God's acts of redemption shifted toward the background and the observance began to take on the character of a mystery cult (Hellenistic influence?). One result is that the eschatological dimension began to disappear from the celebration of Easter and hence from the celebration of the Lord's Supper. "The liturgy of Easter became a celebration of the Liberator rather than of the liberation."

This development proceeded more rapidly in the East than in the West where more of the original idea was preserved. In the East the divine nature of Christ was heavily stressed. This explains why in the East the Ascension was a bigger feast than in the West. It was used in the Easter season (fifty days after Easter Sunday) to read from the book of Acts and from Revelation. The Roman tradition tended to stress the readings from the Gospel of John.

From A.D. 350 onward, there was a season of forty days before Easter. In this arrangement the biblical significance of the number forty played a central role (see the meaning of the forty days or years in the life of Moses, Noah, Elijah, and Jesus). In the West this period is viewed as a time of penitence. Later, in Gaul, the so-called pre-fast arose, the three Sundays that precede the forty-day period and that are known as Septuagesima, Sexagesima, and Quinquagesima. This practice was later adopted by Rome. The forty-day period is also the time of preparation for those who desire to be baptized during the Easter Vigil.

The second cycle in the church year is formed by Christmas and Epiphany, preceded by Advent. Christmas originated rather late and had been known in Rome from around A.D. 330. It is to be understood as the Christianization of the feast of the winter solstice — Christ is the sun of righteousness. Central in the liturgy is Titus 2:11: "For the grace of God has appeared for the salvation of all men . . . awaiting our blessed hope, the appearing of the glory of our great God and Savior Jesus Christ." The sung antiphones that mention the appearance of God in human form are based on Psalm 110. As the feast of Jesus' birth Christmas was adopted by the East from the West, just as in the opposite direction the feast of Epiphany (January 6) came by way of Gaul to the West. In the West the Adoration of the Wise Men came to be the focal point of Epiphany, while the baptism in the Jordan (the focus of Epiphany in the East) and the wedding in Cana were the themes of the two succeeding Sundays. The theme of light permitted a link with Easter. The period of Advent relates to the coming of the Lord and the messianic kingdom — both his first and second comings — hence the readings from Isaiah.

Separate mention needs to be made of the so-called Ember Days — Wednesday, Friday, and Saturday of three (or four) weeks of the year — days of fasting, at the transitions of the seasons in June, September, December, and (later) March. They originated toward the end of the fourth century in Rome. The Ember Days in September are particularly important, because in the liturgy for these days there is an echo of the Jewish autumn festivals. The fact that this character has been preserved is due, in all likelihood, to the absence of a Christian feast in this period. Ember Wednesday reminds us of the Jewish New Year when Psalm 81, the Introitus, summons the liturgist: "Blow the trumpet at the new moon, at the full moon, on our feast day" (v. 3). Hosea 14:1-9, read on Friday, speaks of return and reconciliation and so refers to the Day of Atonement. On Saturday the readings are from Leviticus, the passages concerning the Day of Atonement (23:26-32) and the Feast of Tabernacles (23:39-43); from the letter to the Hebrews about the atonement by Christ the high priest; while the reading from the gospel (Luke 13:6-17) deals with the unfruitful fig tree. A harvest can only come when the life of man bears fruit.

The main service, the service of the Word and Table, everywhere shows in principle the same fundamental pattern. The ministry of the Word consisted of readings from the Old Testament, the letters of the apostles, and the gospel. After the reading of the epistle a psalm was sung. After the exposition the catechumens left, and after the intercessions the service of the Table began. The latter has for its basic pattern eucharistic prayer (known in the East as the *anaphora*, "the prayer offering," in the Roman Catholic tradition as *canon*, and among Protestants as the Communion prayer), the Lord's Prayer, the breaking of bread, and the distribution (communion). The eucharistic prayer itself has a structure of which the Sanctus is a part. In the West (Rome) one notes that the faithful themselves bring forward the gifts of bread and wine. Bread and wine are here the exponents of human existence, the work of our hands, in which believers offer themselves to God. Then, after the gifts of bread and wine — human life — have been offered to God, believers receive them back from the hands of the Lord as the blessed signs of communion with him. Although in this period song gained a secure place in the liturgy, we know next to nothing about the music itself. For some obscure reason, in Rome the readings from the Old Testament disappear from the liturgy.

In the following phrase (from ca. A.D. 600 to 1100), the worship service grew more elaborate and the various traditions mingled (we are now only talking about the West). Gradually, the Roman empire disintegrated and the kingdom of the Franks emerged. Merovingian, Carolingian, and Ottoman kings built up the new empire, whose center of gravity finally came to lie in the region of the Rhine. The original symbolic view of the Eucharist was increasingly subjected to attack and pushed aside by the so-called realistic view, which had an eye only for the physical reality. (Christ is materially present in bread and wine; the words "This is my body" are now interpreted "physically.") This unsalutary development controls the theory of the

Eucharist to this day. Despite political changes, Latin remained the language of the liturgy. In consequence, only the clergy could follow the content of what was taking place in the liturgy and the position of the clergy in the worship service became ever stronger. For believers the language and actions of the liturgy acquired a mysterious character. And although the original Roman liturgy was different, worship in Northwestern Europe became clerical and sacral. The original Gallican liturgy was increasingly Romanized. In time there came into being a conglomerate that could be dubbed a Roman-Frankish-German liturgy. This product was taken by the Ottomans to Rome in the tenth or eleventh century and eventually adopted by the popes. The result was the Western Catholic liturgy.

In this period various liturgical books were joined together, a process ending in the Roman missal. The canonical hours were increasingly made the exclusive domain of the monasteries. The idea gained ground that monks, and later the clergy, must say the prayers, even on behalf of the believers. However, the burden of the daily communal prayers became too heavy for the clergy (increasing involvement with pastoral care). A personal prayer book came into being, one that developed into the Roman breviary. The Scripture readings in the Sunday services were now being fixed and derived mostly from the New Testament. Sometimes the gospel and the epistle readings had some thematic connection, but often there was no link whatever, especially in the case of the Sundays after Pentecost. In the Easter Vigil, following the hymn in honor of the light (the Exsultet), some twelve readings from the Old Testament were given a place. As a result of transferring the Vigil to Holy Saturday, it lost its meaning and effectiveness. A disintegration occurred. Even the celebration of baptism disappeared from the Easter Vigil. It was not restored to its position of honor till 1955.

Over against this, one must recognize that the participation of the people, both visually and corporally, became freer. The liturgy now included a larger number of actions, became more popular and spontaneous, and was less restrained than the original Roman liturgy. The liturgical play, such as the

81

women's visit to the grave, was another new development. In these plays the vernacular was used.

The distance from the official liturgy widened. The symbolic understanding of the liturgy gave way to a more analytic approach. The mystery of the liturgy moved from being a symbol that pointed beyond itself to something incomprehensible and invisible. The bread became the host and was laid upon the tongue of the worshipper (sacralization). Remembering God's saving acts fell further and further into the background. Wegman believes that this development is due to influence from the East that accentuated personal sin and the sense of the holy. The same development came to expression in the architectural arrangement of the church. The altar was moved from the church to the apse where the so-called choir developed. The Eucharist became the Mass. Remembrance in the original sense was replaced by an allegorical approach, a static, moralistic interpretation that is unbiblical and that pushed aside the typology in which the history of redemption, the dynamics of God's action, is central. In succeeding centuries this allegorizing and moralistic approach to the divine acts of salvation became dominant and decisively influenced the outlook and experience of believers.

The period from ca. 1100 to the Council of Trent (1545-1563) was marked by advancing clericalization — believers became spectators. Despite various reform movements — like the Franciscan and that of the Brethren of the Common Life — there is no evidence that these lay movements had any influence on worship. Nor is there any sign of a genuine development of the liturgy. The mood was rather to fix and to guard the tradition. In response to the Reformation, in which an appeal was made to Scripture and to evangelical freedom, the Council of Trent restricted itself to restoring and preserving the existing tradition. Meanwhile, clericalization proceeded further, Latin remained the required language of worship, and uniformity prevailed.

The Roman missal was given its definitive shape. Symbolism weakened even further and the realistic interpretation of bread and wine culminated in the doctrine of transubstantiation, a philosophical rather than a biblical notion.

5. The Approach of the Reformation

The slogan of the Reformation was "back to Scripture." Therefore we must now raise the question whether in the sphere of worship it succeeded in gaining a grasp of the original biblical dimensions and in making them fruitful.

By way of a start we need to admit that the idea of "Scripture alone" is an abstraction. Scripture, itself the product of a process of development, entered the history of the church. By way of a further process of development the church deepened its contact with Scripture, and so the liturgical structures grew. The context in which this process occurred was the Jewish liturgy, and one can clearly trace its path in the Christian liturgy. In returning to Scripture, therefore, one will be obliged to take account of this early tradition. More than this, one is a child of one's own time and cannot simply and without any bias go to "Scripture alone." One reads Scripture through the spectacles of one's own time. One may seek to minimalize this factor, but the obligation to give form to one's association with Scripture in one's own time and culture cannot be avoided.

We must realize that the Reformation took form in the channel of the Renaissance, which, compared to the Middle Ages, was a culture of the intellect. If one were to characterize the Reformation from a liturgical perspective, one could say that liturgy became didactic.[34] It is evident that the Reformation did not primarily aim at liturgical renewal. The liturgical changes that did occur were the result rather of an attempt to go back to Scripture. The service of the Word, in the limited sense of a preaching service, became central. The sacraments, particularly the Lord's Supper, were made almost incidental and lost their place as a focus in the service. Granted, Calvin

34. Ibid., p. 232.

believed that Communion ought to be celebrated weekly, but he was unable to convince his followers of this original Christian datum. The shift from symbol and mystery in the liturgy to an emphasis on doctrine cannot be attributed to a reorientation to the Bible. Instead, it was a reflection of the cultural climate of the day, or, to put it in less friendly terms, an instance of conformity to the world. Not that we ever completely escape conformity, but the striking thing is that at times the world conformity of earlier generations becomes law, a hard rule, for succeeding generations. This is something that can be repeatedly seen in Reformation circles.

At this point, in view of the remarks just made, it is necessary to say a few words about the Reformation, which, culturally speaking, was part of the Renaissance and the Baroque, or of the world of modern thought. If we wish to characterize with a single phrase the development that started with the Renaissance and continues to this day, we may speak of the development of "the mind of science." Accompanying this development is the weakening of a sense of transcendence, of that which transcends the visible world of our experience, and the loss of religious experience.

Medieval man still saw his world as an expression of and a reference to a higher divine order; he was part of a collective structure of experience (cf. the anonymous artist). The Renaissance insisted strongly on the self-consciousness of man. Within the Reformation this new consciousness came to expression in an increased emphasis on a personal relationship to God. The development of self-consciousness was paired with an increasing distance between the inner world and the outer world.

The inner world is the world of consciousness that coincides with what people call the soul; as a result, there originated a religion of inwardness that had little to do with corporeality. The language of the body — kneeling, the procession, the dance, gestures — became irrelevant and is irrelevant for most Protestants to this day.

The exterior world became the world of dead matter, of neutral things valued only on utilitarian grounds. The world or the self is no longer an expression of or a reference to another order. The sense was gradually lost that the earth is full of the glory of the Lord, as for centuries the church had sung of it in the Sanctus. The Sanctus dropped out of the Calvinistic liturgy.

Gradually the idea arose that what cannot be known scientifically is not real. The scientifically knowable became the criterion for determining what was reality. Things lost their referential meaning, their value as symbols, for of course symbolic value cannot be scientifically determined. Theoretical thought increasingly dominated, even in the sphere of the church and the experience of faith. The churches of the Reformation thus increasingly fell victim to the forces of intellectualism and individualism. We shall discuss this issue further in the following chapter. Here we shall restrict ourselves to this brief characterization of the climate in which the liturgy of the Reformation developed.

Of the Reformers Luther was the most traditional, whereas in Calvin, Zwingli, and Bucer the influence of modern thought was clearly visible. A common characteristic was the introduction of the vernacular, and the reading from and interpretation of Scripture. This traditional framework was given a new content. Congregational singing was strongly stimulated and especially aimed at underscoring the message of the sermon. At the same time it expressed the trust in God of a person who knew herself accepted in mercy by God.

The interior of the church building was subjected to radical alteration. The pulpit was put in the center and everything that had to do with images or the imagination was put out. All the emphasis began to fall on the verbal aspect of the services. Kneeling disappeared. Worshippers sat still and listened. Corporeal expression decreased to a minimum. The service became a one-man show. As noted earlier, of all the Reformers Luther stuck closest to the classical tradition. This comes out clearly in his baptismal liturgy in which occurred exorcisms, the giving of salt (symbol of fervency and resistance against evil), the sign of the cross, and the renunciation of Satan. A characteristic feature was the so-called flood-prayer which Luther, with the aid of ancient texts through which the biblical typology came through vividly, probably composed himself.

Whereas in Luther baptism is still an observance that binds human beings to a risen Lord, in the work of the other Reformers the emphasis is upon incorporation into the church. Initially Luther adopted the structure of the Roman mass, abandoning the sacrificial character of the Eucharist and strongly stressing the service of the Word. In his later "Deutsche Messe" Luther offered his own formulations, but kinship with the mass continued to be evident (Kyrie and Sanctus are retained). In Luther the tie between Scripture and table continued. The fixed readings were abolished.

Also in Strasbourg the Reformers built upon the structure of the Mass; a self-formulated order of service followed later. The Lord's Supper's character as an act of thanksgiving (*eucharistia*) was replaced by a didactic and hortatory approach. In this climate Calvin composed his order of service, one deviating from the classic pattern and including, as a noteworthy feature, the Ten Commandments. Although he himself advocated a weekly communion, his followers broke the unity of Scripture and table. The classic system of pericopes listed in the lectionaries was abolished; the *lectio continua*, the practice of reading through entire Bible books, was introduced. The Psalms were made into verse and set to music in four voices. Zwingli, lacking appreciation for symbols and liturgy, abolished all song and music. This was the climate that set the tone for Reformed Protestantism.[35]

Ultimately the reaction of the Reformers and their followers proved as one-sided as the order they opposed. They restored the Word to its central place, but they had little appreciation for symbol or sacrament and failed to find the proper balance between Word and sacrament. A factor in all this is that the Reformers did not know the tradition of the church or the history of the liturgy well. Had they been more familiar with

35. For the orders of service of the Reformers, see J. van der Werf, *Kleine liturgiek.*

86

it, this development would undoubtedly have been different. One cannot in the end even speak of a genuine service of the Word or of Scripture in the churches of the Reformation. The sermon completely dominated the service, in time becoming more argumentative than expository. Lectionaries were not, or hardly ever, used. The worship leader determined what it was that would be read. In practice this turned out to have a very one-sided effect. All forms of church participation other than the singing of the strophic songs disappeared. The church sanctuary literally became an "auditorium."

A favorable exception to this state of affairs is the Anglican liturgy. According to Gregory Dix, it is "the only effective attempt ever made to give liturgical expression to the Reformation principle of justification by faith alone."[36] The celebration of baptism and Communion was renewed, as was the service of the Word, but the liturgy remained continuous with the Catholic tradition. Another striking thing is that the liturgy of the hours, matins and vespers, again became part of the worship of the people.

6. Reorientation

The history of Christian worship reveals that, after an initial spurt of growth controlled by biblical ideas about man and reality, another climate of thought and experience gradually came into being in which the original biblical structures were lost from view. The mind of Greek antiquity played an increasing role in Christian thought. This was true of the Platonist view with its distinction between the visible and the invisible world, the first conceived as pointing to the second. In Augustine this view was given a Christian interpretation. However, the static nature of the distinction brought with it a situation, liturgically, in which the dynamics of redemptive history were suppressed. As a result remembrance, as the central fact of the liturgy, went into eclipse

36. G. Dix, *The Shape of the Liturgy* (London: Dacre Press, 1978), p. 672.

and in the course of time the relationship between symbol and reality became problematic.

The increasing influence of classic modes of thought brought with it the parallel loss of the awareness that Christianity is rooted in Jewish thought. And wherever people failed to realize that Christian worship has its roots in Jewish thought, there was a corresponding increase in the influence of the mind of classic antiquity. The loss of a sense of the Jewish roots of Christian worship was probably the most important factor in the ultimate decline of the liturgy. Certainly we could never in any period withdraw the influence of contemporary culture — we even have to honor fully the questions and problems that arise in that culture. But in this whole process what is decisive is that the original concepts can continue to set the direction of life and worship. Wherever people lose sight of their own roots they are bound to become disoriented.

The desire of the Reformers — Calvin in particular — to return to the original sources was not realized. This can be attributed partly to the nonavailability of the sources needed for reorientation. More important, perhaps, is the fact that succeeding generations did not pursue this course. As a reform movement the Reformation soon came to a dead end. An example of this "dead-endness" is the centuries-long debate between Rome and the Reformers over the issue of the Eucharist, specifically its character as a sacrifice. In retrospect one must say that both parties had lost sight of the original concept. Bread and wine, after all, are brought to the table as symbols or depictions of ordinary daily life, the work of our hands. In these symbols believers offer themselves, their lives and labors, as Paul enjoins Christians to present their bodies (meaning their entire existence) as "a living sacrifice, holy and acceptable to God" (Rom 12:1). In biblical terms a sacrifice is God's gift to man enabling him to draw near to God, as well as a happening by which fellowship among believers is established.[37] At the

37. R. Boon, *Offer, priesterschap, en Reformatie* (Nijkerk: Callenbach, 1966), p. 13.

table we in turn receive bread and wine from the Lord as signs of a new life, a life redeemed by him, as signs of the new fellowship.

Originally, the Eucharist was referred to as "the sacrifice of Christ." By this expression the early church meant the representation of the redemptive work of Christ (remembrance). This has nothing to do with a repetition of the sacrifice of Christ or with a failure to do justice to the uniqueness of the work of Christ. The term is intended to denote the significance of Jesus' sacrifice in the past, the present, and the future.[38]

Neither Rome nor the Reformation seemed to have a clear view of these realities that are so pivotal for the celebration of the Lord's Supper. The practical import of this observation is that the debate between the two was not meaningful and in any case did not lead to the correct view of the issue.

That renewal is necessary hardly needs proof, but clearly attempts at liturgical renewal that proceed solely from the legacy of the Reformation offer little or no hope for the future. Many people are turning away from the Bible and from Christianity without ever having been in essential contact with the pivotal components of life as the Bible sees it.

Evidently renewal must focus on our learning again to deal celebratively with the biblical understandings and perspectives. Without a continuing celebration of God's liberating action, action in which our entire existence is embedded, there is no future for the church. Without this there will be no future, period.

Meanwhile, in our century attempts at renewal have begun. We can only mention here a few of the initiatives taken in the Netherlands.[39] Among Protestants it was J. H. Gunning and A. Kuyper who, at the turn of the century, called for re-

38. Ibid., p. 66.

39. For further orientation, cf. J. F. Lescrauwoet, *De liturgische beweging onder de Nederlandse hervormden in oecumenisch perspectief* (Bussum: Paul Brand, 1957); A. Verheul, *Inleiding tot de liturgie* (Roermond: Romen, 1964), esp. part 2, chap. 3; J. P. de Jong, *De eucharistie — symbolische werkelijkheid* (Hilversum: Gooi en Sticht, 1966).

newed study of the liturgy. Gunning, on grounds of Scripture, took issue with the Zwinglian character of the worship service: the virtual absence of adoration, the neglect of the sacraments, and the view that the sermon is the raison d'être of the service. In his work on worship ("Onze Eredienst") Abraham Kuyper entered a protest against the so-called free inspiration of the preacher. "All liturgy proceeds from the fundamental idea that it is the church which has the minister at its disposal and not vice versa." He characterized a service centered in the sermon, to which prayer and song were then added, as being "contrary to all principles of religion" and "irreligious."[40]

Among other things, Kuyper, who apparently began to reflect on liturgical issues as a result of his encounter with the Anglican liturgy, pleaded for the reintroduction of the practice of kneeling and for the ministry of the "fine arts in the church, on the model of God's ordinances in the Old Testament." In his judgment, though the emphasis on the sermon in the time of the Reformation was understandable, it was nevertheless one-sided and had a disintegrating effect on the church.

Dr. J. H. Gerretsen was one of the first to bring about actual renewal. In 1911, in the Kloosterkerk at the Hague, he introduced a new order of worship in which he strongly stressed the commonality of worship and sought to involve the entire congregation in the action of worship.[41]

Of great significance for the Reformed churches in the Netherlands was the founding, in 1920, of the Liturgical Circle (*Liturgische Kring*) by Dr. G. van der Leeuw. Members of this circle were very active in designing liturgical formularies for the various services (the main service, communion, baptisms, funerals, weddings), in each instance basing their work on the classic texts. Still, in the case of Van der Leeuw, one notes that he devotes more attention to the data from the science and psychology of religion than to the viewpoints of the Bible. This is not to deny that the publication, in 1940, of his book on

40. Cf. Lescrauwoet, *De liturgische beweging*, p. 74.
41. J. H. Gerretsen, *Liturgie* (Den Haag, 1911).

Liturgies ("Liturgiek") was an important contribution to liturgical scholarship.[42] However, the materials he there assembled will only begin to function properly when they are incorporated and interpreted in a biblical framework.

In 1931, at the request of the Liturgical Circle, W. H. van der Pol produced his book on Liturgy (*Liturgie*). In this volume the liturgy is approached in terms of the biblical data and the pre-Reformation tradition and worship are viewed as sacramental. In this study worship is not the place where salvation is talked about but where it is received and experienced. Within Reformed Protestantism the Liturgical Circle initiated the liturgical renewal that was to take shape especially after World War II.

However, the ideas propagated by the Liturgical Circle did stir up criticism. Noordmans especially maintained the classic Reformation positions in which everything hinges on the sermon. And so in Noordmans, "the external word in the worship service became the place of encounter with God. It was especially the spoken or vocal word, while at the same time the sacraments also remained words of some kind."[43] Van der Leeuw's criticism of Noordmans was that he reduced the biblical word to the spoken word but "in Scripture there is more at stake than the vocal word." Noordmans refused to go behind the Reformation, an inherently untenable position because it is not in accordance with Reformation principle.

One could characterize the period before World War II as a time of rehearsals designed to recover the Bible as a liturgical book.

Of great importance among Catholics in this century (ca. 1925) was the work of Dom Odo Casel in the Abbey of Maria Laach.[44] On the basis of biblical and early Christian data he arrived at a new view of the sacrament, in which symbol and reality were no longer opposites but constituted one whole as

---

42. G. van der Leeuw, *Liturgiek* (Nijkerk: Callenbach, 1940).
43. O. Noordmans, *Liturgie*, p. 90.
44. Cf. de Jonge, *De eucharistie*, pp. 33ff.

symbolic reality (cf. chap. 1, sec. 5). His approach was still more Greek than Jewish since his notion of symbol has a Platonic cast. But in any case he does justice to the unity of symbol and reality, a unity denied by modern thought. Van der Leeuw's sacrament theology, which ties in closely with Casel's views, is incorrectly called "Roman Catholic"; "early Christian" would be a better label.

Another person to establish links with the early Christian understanding of symbols was Romano Guardini. For him the central question was how modern humans can recover in actual experience the original meanings and linkages of the Bible.[45] Within this context Guardini also came within earshot of the biblical idea of symbol and tried to overcome an unbiblical and dualistic view of man (the dualistic view that takes man to be a composite of soul and body). It seems that in the tumult of liturgical renewal that followed Vatican II, the work of Casel and Guardini was lost.

After World War II the question seemed increasingly to be how the Bible could function as a liturgical book. Behind this movement, among others, was the person of K. H. Miskotte, who in his own unique way focused attention on the fundamental categories of biblical thought (see also chap. 1, sec. 2). Partly in response to his stimulating influence, a new verification of the Psalms was created and, as an extension of this, a new songbook for the churches ("Liedboek"). [Dr. K. H. Miskotte is known in North America for his book *When the Gods Are Silent*, published in 1967 by Harper and Row, and for *The Roads of Prayer*, published in 1968 by Sheed and Ward.]

In the course of time many "centers for liturgical incubation" came into being in which the Bible functioned as a liturgical book. Here mention must be made of the work of W. Barnard. This poet-theologian again made fluid the crystalline structures of tradition, a stream we may find impossible to

45. Ramano Guardini, *Liturgie und liturgische Bildung* (Würzburg: Werkbund-Verlag, 1966).

chart, but one that "remains a current of living water, the over-flow of the abundance of the Scriptures," as Barnard himself puts it. In his work the typological structures of the Bible surfaced spontaneously, as tradition and poetic creativity formed a lasting covenant.

"The pilgrim never travels alone. Whispers blow his way from the cloud of witnesses, a choir of voices. To this witness of Israel also belongs what the fathers of Christianity have picked up and passed on. They were no angels, and we are not the shepherds of Bethlehem. But they were receptive in times which probably had a better ear than we for the poetic (inter)relationships existing among the separate books of the Bible, for the mystical coherences of meaning between the Law and the Prophets, the Apostles and the Evangelists."[46] Barnard believes that it is the task of the churches of the Reformation to serve as "couriers between Jerusalem and Rome" or, to change the figure, "forever and anew to be the hypotenuse between the base of Scripture and the upright of tradition."

Under the heading of "reorientation," I must not fail to mention a great harvest of new songs that appeared after World War II. It must be counted a unique circumstance in the history of the church that a group of poets in a variety of cooperative enterprises, together with composers, contributed so much to making singable again the biblical senses of things and their interconnections.

What all this creative ferment aims for can perhaps best be illustrated by way of the so-called Song of Scripture by Huub Oosterhuis:[47]

Song of Script(ure)

He who made the dry land,
Called people to coherence,

46. "De Adem van het Jaar," *Mededelingen van de Prof. dr. G. van der Leeuwstichting*, 1975.
47. Huub Oosterhuis, "Schriftlied," in *Werkschrift voor leerhuis en liturgie* 3 (Oct. 1982).

Wrote for our protection
His charter of compassion,
And freed us by his hand.

That book in which are penned
Faces, souls, and names,
Their spreading love,
Their passing love,
Their labor pains that never end.

His imperishable testament:
In his death he with us went —
The days of our years,
Though listed for destruction,
For everlasting life are meant.

Script(ure) that sculpts our future,
O name, forever faithful.

3. *Some Anthropological Assumptions*

1. Revelation and Experience

The central datum in a Christian's involvement with Scripture and the pivot on which the life of the church turns is celebration. The history of the temple, the synagogue, and the church makes that fact very clear. In celebration — the corporate act of remembering the mighty acts in which God revealed himself — the past is reactualized. Its focus is what God has done and will do for us, with us, and in us in Jesus Christ. Such celebration is not a matter of taking note of certain historical facts as fodder for the intellect but the experience of the nearness of God.

The word "experience" as we use it here requires further explanation. For too often "revelation" and "experience" are played off against each other. In biblical times, we are told, the direct experience of the presence of God was a rather normal phenomenon. But since biblical revelation has ceased and God no longer reveals himself directly, experience too has come to an end. In some circles people even mistrust all religious experience, for according to them the only thing that matters is the witness to revelation.

Historically, there is admittedly some ground for this mistrust, but we need nevertheless to see the fundamental distortion in that position. True, the criterion for evaluation does not lie in experience itself; revelation is not a derivative of experience. But having said that we haven't said very much. In this regard the Bible is quite plain. It makes very clear that revelation does not function outside of experience. How could it be otherwise? Human experience is a necessary condition and "instrument" for perceiving revelation. (Religious experience must not, of course, be confused with emotionalism.) The mistrust of religious experience we have noted, sometimes assuming the form of a phobia, appears to be a product of a Western intellectualism marked by spiritual anemia.

People frequently point out the dangers of psychologizing and mention the ideas of Carl G. Jung as illustration.[1] In Jung religion is a matter of experience; that is, it is associated with a consciousness that has been changed by experience of the numinous (the numinous is that which is holy, apart from ethical or rational components). For humans God is not primarily a theological concept but an experience. That is not to say that in Jung God is merely a psychic process in the subconscious. When reference is made to God as an archetype one must realize, says Jung, that the term "type" is derived from the Greek word "typos," which means blow, impression, or image. An archetype presupposes one who produces the impression. From a religious point of view the emphasis is on "the one who impresses"; in psychology, as the only thing within its competence, the emphasis is on the impression. On religion itself Jung has a very positive view. In his judgment, the absence of religion in adults is the chief cause of psychic disorders. Religion is essential to mankind. Psychology must not attempt to explain religion; rather, it should attempt to make clear how people react to religious situations. In Jung, experience does not operate at the expense of revelation. The point is that as a science psychology cannot say anything about revelation.

1. Cf. C. G. Jung, "Jung and Religious Belief," in *Psychology and Western Religion* (Princeton: Princeton University Press, 1984), pp. 255ff.

We must realize in all this that intense religious experiences are relatively rare and were so also in Bible times. By "experience" we mean experience that has been "lived through" with one's entire human existence; it is experience in which the intuitive and affective components have been given their full due. This is not to overlook the intellectual or rational, but these are instrumental parts of the whole, not autonomous functions. When the subject is revelation — not as a theological concept but as a manifestation — this "lived-through" experience is assumed. "That which is experienced is that which comes to us as revelation, that which is disclosed to us. A person can only prepare herself for this event, to receive that which comes as a present."[2] Revelation and experience presuppose one another and stand in a reciprocal relationship. This is very clear from the Sinai stories as recorded in Exodus and Numbers. Israel entered the wilderness to prepare for revelation. To enter the wilderness is a picture of dying to oneself, of purifying oneself, with a view to receiving revelation. By the ritual washing of their clothes and abstaining from sexual intercourse the Israelites engaged in self-preparation (a form of focusing one's attention). The succeeding account of the event of revelation is overwhelming (Ex. 19): it is full of smoke and fire, of flashes of lightning and the sounding of trumpets. On the one hand, the people were filled with dread; on the other, their desire to approach the mountain was so strong that they needed to be held back. When sometime later new experience was delayed, the revelation that had been received was repressed by their own religious projections and the golden calf took shape. Their minds were closed. But that was retrogressive; it led to nothing. What is needed is an open mind: experience must orient itself to revelation.

The same thing emerges from the story of Moses' plea to be allowed to see God (Ex. 33:18-23). Moses got to see God — but not his face; that would have been too much for a human

2. J. Witkam, "Ervaring en openbaring," in *God ervaren?* vol. 2 (Kampen: Kok, 1981), p. 48.

being. Moses only got to see God's back. One can only follow him. Experience takes second place to revelation and must adjust itself to it.

There is always tension between revelation and experience, for revelation is always larger than our capacity to embrace it. People can prepare themselves by turning inward and becoming serene and empty — it is the way of expectation. Revelation on Mount Sinai issued in the giving of the Ten Commandments, "ten steps cut out on the path of mankind to keep it from stumbling."

Preceding this shaping of human life is the experience of God. But for modern man to acknowledge this order of precedence is hard work. Our inclination is rather to ignore our experiences — if we allow them to occur at all — and to make revelation over into a system for us to cling to. We lose our openness, and revelation fails to occur. There is a reciprocal (negative) effect. Without the knowledge of God there is no knowledge of the self (Calvin), but without self-knowledge I will not learn to know God and surrender to him (Augustine).

In this regard we may wish to recall the expression "the fear of God" as it is used in Proverbs 9:10. "The fear of the LORD is the beginning of wisdom." In this expression there are two components: the experience of God's revelation and the experience of surrender to God — a mental process and an encounter. But God is not an extension of man. He remains The Other; he will never be superseded. "The fear of the Lord" as the point of departure for wisdom is characteristic for the whole of biblical revelation.[3] However, wherever revelation is forced into the harness of a system and where dogmas intended as symbols degenerate into conceptual pronouncements, people arrive at the experience of revelation only with great difficulty.

In such a situation it is not at all strange that people begin to look for a point of departure in human experience itself. After all, they reason, in the issue of how to become more human the stories of the Bible can broaden and deepen one's experience.

3. Ibid., p. 52.

Although this is true and generally gets much too little attention, one does run the risk of creating a concept of God based on one's own needs and meeting one's own standards.

From a biblical perspective, the point of departure does not lie in the story of one's own life. The precise opposite is the case. The stories in which the biblical authors have enshrined their deepest experiences — their experience with the name — offer a view of our life stories and give direction to them. "In Scripture you meet God via people. The subject is God; but at the same time the reference is to yourself. I myself am part of the story. The uniqueness of the stories is that they must grow on you and you have to live in them. Perhaps not alone. For that reason we must read the Bible together. The idea is that we start reading. We must come close enough to hear what it says."[4]

It is in the fellowship of faith, particularly the celebrating communities of faith, that the experience of revelation assumes form. The broad complex of experiences that in time grows from involvement with Scripture is passed on in the church. In terms of this tradition, this broad framework of experience, one can then test, deepen, and correct one's own experience. What is essential is that the process of community experience forms one's frame of reference.[5]

The question is how this functions in the worship service. Before discussing this question we must underscore that "the house of celebration" cannot stand by itself. It must be accompanied by "the house of study" and "the house of service." They presuppose one another. In "the house of study" the accent lies on gaining insight into the biblical connections and backgrounds and on their effect in the concreteness of human existence. Instruction, analysis, and argument all play their role in the process.

But in "the house of celebration" the accents are clearly

4. G. D. J. Dingemans, "Openbaring en ervaring in de catechese," in *God ervaren?* vol. 2 (Kampen: Kok, 1981), p. 65.
5. Ibid., p. 71.

different. Analysis and argument do not belong here. Here the stories are handed down. Miskotte, for one, has entered a plea for the restoration of storytelling. The story is a form of proclamation. We need to be delivered from the illusion that the story, after all, is just a tale and that the message can be reduced to a few main concepts. It is God who causes the story of what he has done to go from mouth to mouth and from generation to generation. The story as the vehicle of truth carries it forward.[6]

Biblical stories are future-oriented. Recollection of the promises, not recollection as such, is central. In the present, too, the promises can enter a new phase of fulfilment. In the context of worship the idea is not simply to relate the old stories; the idea is to pass on the stories, stories situated in tradition but open to the future, stories that form the framework of interpretation for our own experiences, both common and personal. This implies that in the biblical stories we recognize features of our own life; we relate to them in ways that go beyond mere interpretation. The images become examples, and we are urged forward.

For a vital experience to occur in the worship service, two conditions must be met. In the first place, one needs to become familiar with the stories and the tradition to which he belongs. If one is not really familiar with them, they cannot function as a framework of interpretation. This means that study, in the church, the family, and the school, is indispensable. Storytelling in and around the church must abound, but always in the context of the tradition of the church, and not in terms of the pious chitchat that sometimes surfaces in child story Bibles.

In the second place, the story must be told in such a way that the connection with our own world of experience is made. The process begins by reading the story well, for the manner of public reading is the beginning of interpretation. The images that are basic to the story must come alive in a new imaging.

6. K. H. Miskotte, *When the Gods Are Silent* (New York: Harper and Row, 1967), pp. 199-207.

This imaging need not be limited to the spoken word. Music, dance, movement, and pictorial representation all have the potential for enlarging and deepening the possibilities of experience. But the story remains the central datum.

In passing, it may be useful to mention the misunderstanding that telling stories is something only for (little) children. This prejudice is the ripe fruit of Western intellectualism, which only regards as fully valid an abstract and conceptual approach. But that tide is now turning and so-called narrative theology has restored the story to its central position.[7]

The story in the biblical tradition — "he said nothing to them without a parable" — was continued in the Jewish tradition. Martin Buber has this to say on the subject: "The words used to describe these experiences were more than mere words; they transmitted what had happened to coming generations, and with such actuality that the words in themselves became events. And since they serve to perpetuate holy deeds, they bear the consecration of holy deeds."[8] In the same context Buber tells of a rabbi who believed that one should tell a story in such a way that the teller is swept along by it himself. Said the rabbi: "My grandfather was lame. Once they asked him to tell a story about his teacher. And he related how the holy Baal Shem used to hop and dance while he prayed. My grandfather rose as he spoke, and he was so swept away by his story that he himself began to hop and to dance to show how the master had done. From that hour on he was cured of his lameness. That's the way to tell a story!"

In chapter 1 we already noted that the biblical stories are not self-contained historical events. This is an essential datum when the subject is revelation and experience. The Bible tells us of things that continue to happen. To limit Scripture to the past by reducing it to reportage and to think of it as a picture

7. For an introduction to narrative theology, cf. Bernd Wacker, *Narrative Theologie?* (München: Kösel, 1977).

8. Martin Buber, *Tales of the Hasidim: The Early Masters* (New York: Schocken, 1947), p. v.

montage in writing is to make it void and mute for life in the present and the future. Reading the Bible in the worship service — passing on the story — should lead people to faith, to the awareness that our own existence constitutes a part of the story. In other words, the Bible has to be lived. "A complete revelation occurs only, therefore, when a vital connection is made between Scripture (the tradition of faith) and the reality accessible to us."[9]

This is how the Bible must function in the liturgy. The life of Jesus, the incarnate Word, makes this clear to us. In Scripture and particularly in the Psalms he recognized the shape of his own life. Psalm 22 became his own story, the story of passing from death into life. In a similar fashion we must allow ourselves to be instructed by the stories and the Psalms in order to recognize the shape of our own lives and to allow ourselves to be directed — to live before the face of God.

Blessings to You

I walked and talked with the Lord.
We walked side by side,
The Father and the child
who does not yet understand.
She barely dared ask a question.

With the dew still on the ground
We started out:
He took me by the hand.

The flowers greet him
Yet, Lord — the bashful brook
Almost stops its gurgling
The mountains begin to glow.

We walk side by side,
the Father and the child.

9. H. Renckens, "Richtlijnen voor bijbellezen," in *Werkschrift voor leerhuis en liturgie* 1 (1981): 52ff.

I do not see him but he
is closer to me
than any earthly being ever was.

(Ida Gerhardt, collected poems)[10]

The liturgy is service — to God and to one another; it is
the place where we sing of hope and the future; it is where
people are swept along by the vision of the coming kingdom.
"To listen to what is behind and to look at what is ahead" —
that, says Oosterhuis, is a possible definition of liturgy. But all
that is directly bound up with our experience, with the entire
fabric of existence. Clearly, experience cannot in this connection
be equated with feeling, as is sometimes done. Of course, the
two cannot be isolated from each other either, but experience
is much broader and is of a different order. Among other things,
knowing and imaging also belong to it.

Whenever there is talk of religious experience — and in a
biblical climate such talk relates to a self-revealing God — there
is reference to a meaning that though associated with observable phenomena transcends those phenomena. Within this context of revelation and the ascription of meaning, one can speak
of religion as a trust relationship in which the whole person is
involved, not just that person's feelings. Religious experience
arises in the confrontation with the transcendent, with the
Other who reveals himself. One might also speak of religious
perception. In those cases where people follow up on this experience and enter into relationship with it, a relationship of
trust comes into being and one can speak of "the experience of
faith."[11] The Hebrew word for faith, *emuna*, clearly points in
this direction; it refers to trust in the Other, a fellowship of life
or personal fellowship with God. Buber spoke of the I-Thou
relationship.

All this also has something to do with finding one's own

10. Ida Gerhardt, *Verzamelde gedichten* (Amsterdam: Polak en Van
Gennep, 1980), p. 341.
11. J. Weima, *Reiken naar oneindigheid* (Baarn: Ambo, 1981).

identity. Who am I and how do I find fulfilment? And of course, our identity goes far beyond the things that occur to us consciously. The whole of our life, says Dorothy Sölle, is founded in the mystery of the absolute.[12] God knows us more deeply than does anyone else. Each person is a mystery that, though it cannot be solved by one's involvement with Scripture, can be made transparent by it. In this involvement the question of Psalm 139 recurs:

> Search me, O God, and know my heart!
> Try me and know my thoughts!
> And see if there be any wicked way in me,
> And lead me in the way everlasting!

This is not a matter for the individual only. The words are always mediated by the community of faith. Celebrating the liturgy both establishes and presupposes community. Where community is weak — and unfortunately in the church that is the rule rather than the exception — this mediation, like the process of identification, proceeds only with great difficulty. Under these conditions the mystery of existence only becomes transparent against great odds.

A person's "religiousness" manifests itself in the longing for salvation, for wholeness, for a life without fear, a life in which trust is the basis of one's happiness. The story of God and his world, the story that is transmitted in worship, gives direction to that longing and unites a person with his own inwardness. In cases where people do not (yet?) know that longing, they are more likely to seek in worship a confirmation of their own closed world, their egocentricity. Some writers (Rümke, for instance) then speak of a "developmental disturbance." The inability to experience longing, the absence of imaginative power, the habit of being led by standards of utility and efficiency — they are all of them signs of religious underdevelopment, of a life on a "flat one-dimensional plane." There

---

12. Dorothee Sölle, *Death by Bread Alone* (Philadelphia: Fortress Press, 1978), pp. 95ff.

is neither future nor hope in such an outlook. A problem at least as large is that the usual liturgical orders are too restricted; one might say, they are not prophetic enough to give shape to that longing and to make possible the journey back into responsibility in the midst of the world (Dorothy Sölle).

Still, in every liturgical celebration not only the "journey outward" will have to be present, but also the "journey inward," finding one's own identity in the encounter with God. One can find this structure in many stories in Scripture. A classic example, as Sölle points out, is the story of Elijah on Mt. Horeb. "Arise and eat, else the journey will be too great for you," says the angel of the Lord (1 Kings 19:7). The journey is the classic image of the development of one's own inner experience. The journey inward, described as the loss of self and the finding of a new self, follows several stages: the strong wind, the earthquake, the fire, and finally the sound of "the still small voice." God does not manifest himself in the (natural) powers of this world, nor does Elijah experience in them the deepest foundation or mystery of his existence. But these images do not only represent the powers of nature. The storm — says an old interpretation — also represents Elijah's rebellion, the earthquake his uncertainty, and the fire his fear. At the sound of the "still small voice" Elijah wraps his face in a mantle. Literally, the text refers to him as "freezing" at the high penetrating sound. The expression denotes the deepest depths of despair, in which fear passes into insensitivity — the rigidity of death. It is at this low point that God appears to Elijah and he can talk again. Then the journey outward begins. The Lord speaks to him: "Go, return . . ." (1 Kings 19:15). The prophetic mandate, with its clear political implications, is renewed.

For several hundred years now Protestants have had a hard time finding the journey inward, finding their own identity in relation to revelation; and they no longer have a clear view of the journey outward. Where people have trouble with the political implications of the gospel something is also likely the matter with their spirituality. The longing for wholeness is also a longing for new community, for a future in which God is "all in all." It is the future now celebrated, in sign language, by the community of faith. In Scripture this perspective is presented in the image of the wedding feast. And the longing for wholeness comes to expression in the celebration of the Lord's Supper.

However, our subjectivism and individualism make it next to impossible for us to gain a clear view of the totality of things and so to experience unity and community. Identity and totality constitute the twin pillars of religious experience. But both experiences barely come to any development in our culture because they are no longer nurtured by adequate immersion in Scripture. This lack of development is the result especially of the historicizing approach to the Bible we discussed in chapter 1. The attempt to reduce truth to the question whether something "really" happened or not is unacceptable and degrades "remembrance" to mere mental recall. In the context of commemoration and recall there is little or no room for the dimensions of experience in question. And where "the journey inward" stagnates "the journey outward" cannot take shape. One of the most important goals of liturgical renewal is the effort to bring the two journeys into alignment.

Being baptized with Christ we die and rise again to a new life, accepting the responsibility for the journey outward. Having been justified we now pursue justice, "always abounding in good works."

Religion creates a certain distance from concrete reality. In that posture there is, besides wonder, a critical element that motivates people to break out of their confinement within overly narrow limits. But this dynamic element also has been repressed in Western culture. Wherever the dynamic structure of remembrance disappears, liturgy begins to confirm the status quo.

Sometimes "spirituality" and "solidarity" appear to be opposites. Now and then, however, people succeed in restoring the original unity. The intentional communities that find their focus in the deliberate practice of the unity of spirituality and solidarity are luminous examples. Action in conformity with the Torah and the Gospel can only take shape when it is fed and directed from within fellowship with God. One of the best-known examples is the community of Taizé.[13]

Celebration and willingness to serve presuppose order and discipline. Discipline has to do with discipleship, in freedom choosing a life of service. "Spirit and body are one. To keep them open, at God's disposal, is the basis of inner discipline. The goal is to keep the creature in communion with the Creator. The only perspective is the kingship of Jesus Christ over the whole person," says Roger Schutz, founder and prior of the community of Taizé.[14] Acting under the impulse of good intentions without a deeper spiritual foundation can easily derail a person and do more harm than good to one's neighbor. Needed for a genuinely useful life are training and discipline nurtured by community with God and one's neighbor.

In Taizé — whose members are involved in all kinds of ways in aid to others, going as far as South and Central America — this belief has assumed form, for instance, in daily prayers: morning, midday, and evening prayers. Through these means the members are inspired and energized to be able to do all their work. At this point it is worth noting how the Psalms are used in the daily prayers. They are sung by a soloist while the congregation sings the antiphons. The object is to bring out that the Psalms are not primarily the expression of the feelings of the church but the prayers of the Messiah. This belief ties in with the understanding of ancient Israel.

In this context one must realize that the regular evening sacrifice in Israel was devoted to the remembrance of Passover where the Passover lamb is the image of the sacrifice of the Messiah. The object of prayer is, therefore, not in the first place to experience the power of prayer but to seek communion with Christ, who himself prays for us. In Taizé dimensions of prayer

13. See, for instance, Rex Brico, *Taizé, Brother Roger and his Community* (London: Collins, 1978).
14. P. O. Elderenbosch, *De rivier die in Taizé ontspringt* (Nijkerk: Callenbach, 1975), p. 60.

107

have been discovered that had been lost from view in the course of time. And this life of prayer has proven to be a direct source of inspiration for concrete action. "It is incomprehensible," says Elderenbosch, "that there is not much more prayer in our churches, considering that the position of a church community which takes God's mandate seriously is not different from that of the community of Taizé."[15]

What was surprising was that many people were able to pray in Taizé who could not do so in their environment at home. Here they discovered something of the Spirit who prays for us.

The search for communion with Christ and service to the world constitutes a single whole. But this unity was increasingly lost sight of, the more conceptual theology and intellectual insight began to dominate. Correspondingly, the experience of faith became ever more attenuated. But in a truly Christian life, so Taizé would teach us, spirituality and solidarity, liturgy and responsible social action, go together. In such a life people again experience the impact of revelation, and discover the meaning of the words: "Speak, LORD, for thy servant hears" (1 Sam. 3:9).

2. Human Beings Are Their Bodies

We have asserted repeatedly that liturgy is not merely a "spiritual" issue but one that concerns the entire person, soul and body. Now, the interpretation of these terms — "spirit," "soul," "flesh," and "body" — as they occur in Scripture, is a story by itself. Rather soon in the history of the church, however, these terms were interpreted in the light of Greek thought — with all the consequences this entailed. Whereas in the Bible human corporeality was viewed very positively (after all it is the Creator who gave this form to human existence), in the early church, under the dominance of Greek thought, the body was soon viewed as the lower part of a human being and a big drag

15. Ibid., p. 24.

on the immortal soul. To many Christian people, sexuality especially was proof of human perversity.

This dualistic view of man, in which the soul was the higher and the body the lower part, for centuries had its ill effect on Christianity, and we are still picking its bitter fruits. Many people even think that this view is biblical! But for liturgical celebration a consistent application of this dualistic view spells death. Celebration, then, is something for the "inner man," something that does not involve the body. Real remembrance and celebration of the great festivals becomes impossible on this view. Hence it is of fundamental importance to recapture a biblical view of man.

To begin, it must be noted that the Old Testament does not have the familiar distinction between body and soul as two separate entities. The words "soul" and "flesh" overlap. Human beings are "souls" and they are "flesh," not a composite of both. The differences between the two are differences in viewpoint. "Soul" is vitality, the locus of emotion, and often denotes the entire person. So the Old Testament speaks of souls that are hungry, and of Noah and his eight souls. There is no inner world that opposes an outer world, no inner soul as opposed to a body in the outer world. Thought, intention, and act are together one unit.

Flesh is almost synonymous with soul, as when we read: "My soul longs . . . for the courts of the LORD; my heart and flesh sing for joy to the living God" (Ps. 84:2). Flesh is a reference to the entire person, but here as something perishable. Hence body and flesh do not denote anything spatial, as we think of. The reference is to a quality, particularly a quality in relation to God, as perishability implies a situation before the face of God.[16]

According to Shalom Ben Chorin, the Song of Solomon is the most striking expression of the unity between body and soul.[17] In the Song of Solomon a person's corporeality is ac-

16. C. S. van Peursen, *Lichaam, ziel, en geest* (Utrecht: Bijleveld, 1978).
17. Shalom Ben Chorin, *En schiep hen naar zijn beeld* (Baarn: Ten Have, 1973).

cepted without reservations. And that includes the erotic fire belonging to it. In this connection Shalom Ben Chorin also mentions that the Hebrew does not have the Greek distinction between eros and agape. Love (*ahabah*) is indivisible and is a power of God.

> . . . For love is strong as death,
> jealousy is cruel as the grave.
> Its flashes are flashes of fire,
> a most vehement flame (or flame of the Lord).
>
> Song of Sol. 8:6

(The flashes of fire are the flames of revelation, the flames manifest in love, according to the past.)

A symbolic understanding of the Song of Solomon does not imply the suspension of its concrete eroticism as though it were meant only allegorically. Nor does the idea that events on earth adumbrate events in heaven imply a suspension of those earthly events. The opposite is true. The reality of the earthly events is presupposed.

"The body," says Shalom Ben Chorin, "is the parable of the soul which is manifest in it, but not its adversary."

An important point in the biblical view of the body is the role it assigns to the senses. H. W. Wolff has pointed out that in the Old Testament a person's face is much more important than his head,[18] the reason being that the organs of communication — the eyes, the mouth, and the ears — are located in the face. A special place is accorded to the ears and mouth, because it is through them that communication with God takes place. Humans are distinguished from the rest of creation by the faculty of speech. The mouth speaks what the ear hears. Singing again has special place, certainly when it concerns involvement with the words of Scripture. In singing a person rises above herself: speech and silence achieve a higher unity. Sensory and motor abilities belong together. There is no such thing as ob-

18. H. W. Wolff, *Anthropologie des Alten Testaments* (München: Kaiser, 1973).

110

2. Human Beings Are Their Bodies

servation in passive isolation. To mention the body and the senses is to speak at the same time of corporeal expression.

It has often been said that the Hebrews were "auditory" and the Greeks "visual" in their approach to life; this must not be construed to mean, however, that the Hebrew approach was nonvisual! Certainly the accents were not the same, but anyone studying the celebration of the Feast of Tabernacles in the temple at Jerusalem will soon come to the conclusion that seeing plays an important role in it. In Proverbs we read: "The hearing ear and the seeing eye, the LORD has made them both" (20:12).

The Bible is free from prejudice against the bodily experience, an experience and acceptance that is basic to the liturgical celebration in which sensory and motor skills are totally included. Experience is a central component here because celebration is totally absorbing, involving all parts of a person.

It is not a simple matter for us to find our connections with this biblical language of the body: from its very beginnings Western culture was marked by a dualism of body and mind (or spirit).

This dualism was further accentuated when in the seventeenth century Descartes identified "soul" (*geest*) with human consciousness, an identification that further increased the gap. The distance between "soul" on the one hand, and affectivity and vitality on the other, was maximized. This distance was initially a matter of theory, but in time it entered into the experience of Western man. Reactions to this split were initially even more one-sided — like the reductions to spiritualism, idealism, materialism, and vitalism. The dichotomy between "spirit" and "matter" has been carved deeply into Western man, so deeply in fact that any mention of the original unity always bears traces of the dichotomy. Our language barely permits us to talk differently, as is evident from a term like "animated corporeality" that seeks to do justice to the unity.

It is self-evident that these factors have a profound influence on the liturgy. It is still necessary to posit the thesis that

111

worship is the meeting with God of the whole person. Admittedly, present-day anthropology has made progress in its attempts to overcome the dichotomy. But one still encounters strong resistance when, in a liturgical context, the human body comes up for discussion in other than minimal terms. In the newer positions the body has become more than an instrument; instead of "I have a body" one hears it said that "I am my body." The spiritual existence of human beings is expressed in their corporeality, in posture and movement, in facial expression and body language. At stake is a single reality — the one being of a person.

This view spells the end of the absolute supremacy of the conscious mind. It is often said that a person is able to enter into contact with another through the body. This is correct, provided the contact is not limited to the conscious mind. For even before there is any consciously focused attentiveness for another person, there can be a relationship on an unconscious or preconscious level. This is a good thing, for otherwise the communication would have a very one-sided cerebral character.

We are often barely conscious of the affective dimensions that play a large role in the liturgy, but they inevitably do. Ultimately, and probably even less so today than in the past, we are unable to put our deepest experiences in words. This works better in dimensions other than the verbal, as, for example, in artistic productions. But these are not accessible to all. Still, there always remains a hidden element that may be sensed but cannot be disclosed. The reality of our corporeality at its deepest levels is rooted in the fact of creation and in being included in Christ's resurrection — the Easter mystery. The early church accorded much significance to the body, as appears from its celebration of the sacrament of baptism. Totally naked and with loosened hair, in order to bring the entire body in contact with the water of baptism, the baptized entered the water both to be submerged and to rise again. Thereupon the body was anointed as a sign of the total consecration of human existence. In this process, and in principle, the body shares in the glorification that is part of the consummation.[19]

Essential to one's corporeality is action. Liturgical actions are called rites. The rite is on the same level as the symbol (cf. chap. 1, sec. 4); it is a concrete action and can therefore be designated as a symbolic action. A distinguishing feature of the rite is repetition.[20] Daily life, too, has its rituals, such as rituals of greeting in various situations. Children, especially, are sensitive to fixed patterns of action.

The evening prayer in the (ancient) church is a ritual of preparation for the night. The idea of ritual is to ascribe meaning to one's daily existence; by the repetition of the ritual a relationship to a deeper reality than the immediate one of sight and sound is established. Not, of course, that we have in mind a mechanical action or sterile ceremony. Dedication and imaginative self-involvement are essential.

Liturgical rites form part of actual remembrance. Detached from remembrance they lose their significance. Modern thought, unfortunately, has as little appreciation for rites as for symbols: "It is *just* a ritual or *only* a symbol." The result is that modern life has become barren and we hardly know what to do with important events in our lives. This is particularly apparent from our awkward mumblings at deaths, funerals, or other times of grief.

The same is true for our "communion" with God. In the absence of rituals our important experiences cannot be assimilated, worked through, or expressed. And to work through them is more than talking about them. Ultimately, we humans cannot manage without rites and, accordingly, one observes in church and society a search for new forms in order, by means of symbolic actions, to achieve contact with deeper realities. So-called "experiments" as a rule prove to have stronger ties

19. A. Verheul, *Inleiding tot de liturgie* (Roermond: Romen, 1904), p. 134.
20. G. Lukken, *De onvervangbare weg van de liturgie* (Hilversum: Gooi en Sticht, 1980), pp. 16ff.

with the past than one would expect upon first encountering them. Often these "experiments" are ancient ideas dressed in new finery.

Ritual, one must know, has a broader meaning than rite. Symbol, rite (symbolic action), and words together constitute a ritual. Words are more than concepts because they evoke and unveil reality. In English, as in other languages, "saying" is related to "seeing," "to cause to be seen."[21] The reference here is to what Oosterhuis calls a second language. It is not the language of objective information and of concepts but a language of imagery, of poetry. The language used in ritual is a "second language," the language of the liturgy. When in baptism the minister or priest says "I baptize you," he is not just making a statement but performing the act of baptism. Something is effected. To tear these things apart, to contrast word and rite and symbol, is bad business — the result of secularized thought. Every component of a ritual has its own meaning but is at the same time conditioned by the whole of the ritual. Nonverbal action has a deeper reach, but because it is more vague it calls for the language of denotation. "One could say that symbols and rites give us the space and time of human life but that the words define them as *this* particular meaningful and salvific event here and now" (Lukken). It is hard to conceive of faith apart from ritual. Experiences must be named and given form.

3. Corporeality and Expression

Liturgical rituals are the framework that shape the world of the believer's experience. Two aspects must be distinguished. On the one hand, there is the connection with the revelation of God; witness comes alive and proclamation takes place. On the other hand, the framework provides an opportunity for response. The believer expresses his act of surrender to the Lord

21. Ibid., p. 24.

and praises his name. Though proclamation and expression constitute two distinct aspects, the two cannot be separated. Where expression does not develop, the proclamation cannot prosper. Also, where corporeality was either undervalued or suppressed, the expression of faith was reduced to a minimum. The most noteworthy characteristics of the worship service were, and often still are, sitting still and listening.

In the early twenties Guardini already expressed the opinion that necessary liturgical renewal would not occur if its advocates limited themselves to the renewal of texts and music. In his opinion, the dimension of movement is indispensable to liturgical celebration.[22] This, to him, was something much bigger than letting the congregation participate. He raised the question of how, for example, walking in a procession could become a religious act, the act of accompanying the Lord as he traverses the land, an act in which the encounter with the Lord could take place. Thus, walking forward to the table is not only a matter of movement but a symbolic action expressing surrender and the willingness to serve. Doing things is centrally significant. "Action is an elementary thing in which the whole person must put herself with all her creative powers; it must be the performance of a vital act; a living experience, a living understanding, an Act of seeing." Guardini made the attempt to revive the ancient language of gesture that is rooted in Bible times. The dimension of movement not only concerns gesture; it also concerns the dance.

In the Old Testament the liturgical dance is fully incorporated as a valid act. Although it was never officially adopted in worship, the liturgical dance continued as a practice here and there right into the Middle Ages. To this day, in the church of Sevilla, what is called "the dance of the angels" is performed around the altar by ten boys three times a year. However, as in the course of centuries appreciation for bodily expression waned, dancing had to be abandoned. Finally, at the Council

22. R. Guardini, *Liturgie und liturgische Bildung* (Würzburg: Werkbund-Verlag, 1966).

of Würzburg (1298), the liturgical dance was declared to be a serious sin. Still, the church never quite succeeded in banishing it. In the Pentecost liturgy in Santiago, Chile, dance, rhythm, and emotional expression remained central.

Meanwhile, corporeality has been rediscovered, as has the symbolism of movement. Especially as the result of more intensive contact with other cultures, people in the West have gained appreciation for this dimension. However, this rediscovery still has to affect the liturgy. Whereas initially the counterargument was that movement and dance ran counter to the tenor of Western culture, now there is talk of impoverishment and the necessity of learning to take advantage of these possibilities. This ground swell runs parallel to the increased emphasis on the unity of soul and body. To the degree that that unity is experienced again, movement and dance will also emerge as primary functions of life.

The reverse is also true. In the dance, the "boundary lines" between soul and body are gone; soul and body interpenetrate. The dance provides a total experience of reality; all things are caught up in it. The experience can be so intense that it is said that the rivers clap their hands, mountains skip for joy like rams and the hills like lambs, as is the case in some of the Psalms (Ps. 114:6, for example).

In any case, the rediscovery of our corporeality has opened our eyes to the biblical reality of praising God with the body. In rabbinical literature there is frequent reference to Psalm 35:10: "All my bones shall say, 'O LORD, who is like thee?' " The bones in question are the vertebrae of the backbone, which sways or moves with the prayers in a Jewish worship service. In this connection M. A. Beek refers to a prayer in the sabbath morning liturgy.

> For all this the tongue thou hast placed in our mouth, the limbs with which thou hast endowed us, and the spirit and soul thou hast breathed into us, all shall acknowledge, bless, praise, glorify, extol, sing, sanctify, and declare thy sovereignty, our King. Yea, every mouth shall give thee

praise, every tongue shall pay thee homage, every knee shall bend to thee, and all that is upright shall bow down before thee. All hearts shall revere thee and all our innermost being shall chant thy praise, even as the psalmist sings: "All my bones shall say, O LORD, who is like thee?"[23]

The word "bones" is often linked with the palm branch in the *lulab*, which is carried around and swung during the Feast of Tabernacles. The bending of the palm branch is an image of the bending of one's backbone. The Hebrew words for prayer are all associated with words like standing, kneeling, or prostrating oneself, and thus suggest a close relationship between prayer and corporeal expression.

After discussing these and other data from the Old Testament and the Jewish liturgy, and raising the question of what the implications of this material are for present-day worship, Beek remarks:

> The question remains whether our common worship is not seriously impoverished when our bodies in the pews are not given any space for purposes other than to sit or to stand. As long as perfect silence remains the height of our liturgical ambition when the Word is heard, so that the dropping of a penny or the cry of a child turns into an incident, the house of prayer will not be a real home to us. As long as this ideal prevails, genuine liturgical renewal cannot occur and no one will ever, like the poet of Psalm 42, remember that, free from loneliness and distress, he or she used to go with the throng in procession to the house of God, with glad shouts and songs of thanksgiving — a multitude keeping festival! We have surrendered processions to the organizers of political demonstrations and the dance to the exploiters of dance halls and we have barely an idea of what it could mean if in the

23. M. A. Beek, "God loven met het lichaam," in *Loven en geloven* (essays in honor of N. H. Ridderbos) (Amsterdam: Bollard, 1975). The material quoted in translation was copied from *Traditional Prayer Book for Sabbath and Festivals,* ed. David de Sola Pool (New York: Behrman House, 1960), pp. 174-76.

church we could celebrate with dances and sing the Simchat Torah (Rejoicing in the Law).

In this context we must realize that the liturgical dance has in it the element of play (something different from playing games), play that takes place before the face of God. Modern dance, which stresses the individual, often lacks this character of play and does little to create community.

After the rediscovery of human corporeality in the first half of the twentieth century, following World War II there has emerged here and there some interest in the dimension of movement in the liturgy.[24] It was especially G. van der Leeuw who in his book on the relationship between religion and art again emphatically called attention to the role of movement in the religious life.[25] The movement of the body, says Van der Leeuw, often conveys more of the totality and background of life than words or even music is able to do.

More attention is now being given to the anthropological dimension of the faith. This dimension was not absent in the preceding phase, but it was interpreted one-sidedly by the excessive accentuation of humans as rational beings. We are talking now about shifts in perception. In the Western world anthropological "broadening" in worship, the effect of the rediscovery of the dimension of movement, was first manifest in American churches. The song "Lord of the Dance" became very popular.

Dance, then, wherever you may be;
I am the Lord of the Dance, said he,
And I'll lead you all, wherever you may be,
And I'll lead you all in the dance, said he.

This material sounds very modern, but the theme of Christ as Lord of the Dance is an ancient Christian motif. The church fathers already spoke of the heavenly blessedness

24. Carolyn Deitering, *The Liturgy as Dance and the Liturgical Dancer* (New York: Crossroad, 1984).
25. G. van der Leeuw, *Wegen en grenzen* (Paris, Amsterdam, 1932, 1955).

evoked by the dance. In the painting Fra Angelico (ca. 1445) made of the Last Judgment, virgins and martyrs dance a heavenly dance. In various medieval songs, too, we discover the theme of Christ as Lord of the Dance. Now that the urge toward movement in liturgy is returning, the ancient motifs seem to be making a comeback also.

Experiments in movement are also being undertaken in the Federal Republic of Germany. These experiments found a very warm response at a Church Day in Düsseldorf in 1973, when thousands of people, in a night of worship, danced to songs like "He's Got the Whole World in His Hands" and to a sung version of the Lord's Prayer.[26] It still seems a bit strange to us. But "why should humanity not once again speak in its most ancient language of the great mystery of movement and countermovement, the movement that proceeds from God to this earth?" (Van der Leeuw). In our thinking we are stuck with a static image of God; but in biblical revelation movement dominates. God is one who acts and accompanies his people. The dance can remind us of this fact.

In the liturgy, in the proclamation in which God's movement takes place, the church is called to answer and respond. And how else could it respond but by word, music, and gesture? This implies the search for new forms on the basis of tradition. "If liturgy is to be and remain a relevant sign of the redemptive action of Christ, it must enter into dialogue with . . . the people of our time. For a long time both church music and liturgical language were in the forefront of the renewal movement. It seems to me that it is now the turn of the dimension of movement, so that liturgy may truly become a faith expression of the entire person" (Sequeira).

The subject of "movement" in the liturgy has also come up in the Netherlands in the last few years, in regard to both proclamation and the responding congregation. The theologian-dancer Andries Kobus has been active on the track of

26. A. R. Sequeira, "De herontdekking van de bewegingsdimensie in de liturgie," in *Concilium* 16, 2 (1980): 98-103.

proclamation.[27] His question is how the dance as one mode of expression next to other modes can be made serviceable to the proclamation of the Word within the liturgy. "Movement within the breath of God," he calls it. When it is done well it will set people in motion and they will become genuine participants. Kobus enters a plea for a congregational introit, in which everyone in procession comes singing into the church. In another example the liturgist dances the Kyrie while the congregation sings the Gloria.

And this leads to another question. How do we get "a new body for the Lord" and how do we use it?[28] In most cases we are a "sitting" (and well-established) church, and sometimes we even manage to celebrate the Lord's Supper without going to the table by having ourselves served while seated in the pews.

Blankesteijn has made a start by situating the worship service in an almost empty space with a rug in one corner where the smaller children can amuse themselves. The children are part of the church, and we must therefore organize the celebration to involve them. One of the most elementary rules for children at worship is that they have space in which to move. Either standing or sitting on the floor (with a chair here and there for those who cannot stand very well), people follow a service in which the Eucharist has a fixed place. There is no collection, but people bring their gifts to the table, a very ancient practice. In preparing the liturgy provision is made for a processional dance or something like it between the prayer of preparation and the distribution of bread and wine. In this dance, a kind of interpretation of the Lamb of God, people experience the future perspective that belongs to the celebration of Communion. Other patterns of movement are also used.

27. A. Kobus, "De dans heeft lang genoeg gewacht," in *Mededelingen van de Prof. dr. G. van der Leeuwstichting*, no. 53; a conversation about the preceding work between A. Kobus and H. Blankesteijn, in *Rondom het Woord* 22, 3 (1982): 34ff.; A. Kobus, "Bewegen in de adem van God," in *Rondom het Woord* 24, 3 (1982): 18ff.
28. H. R. Blankesteijn, "Een nieuw lijf voor de Heer," a conversation with Y. van der Groot, in *Rondom het Woord* 24, 3 (1982): 2-17.

The striking thing in this context is that everything takes place within the framework of the classic liturgy (introit, Kyrie, Gloria, etc.), which creates the space in which, as it were, the improvisations are kept in place. It is precisely this formal framework, says Blankesteijn, that creates freedom.[29]

4. Creative Imagination

In chapter 1 (sec. 5) we remarked that the language of images that gives us access to the biblical world presupposes in the person hearing it the noetic function of the imagination. The authors of Scripture, says R. Boon, "appeal to our imagination and our associative capacities, to our emotions and to our receptivity to impressions and perceptions. The idea is that images can be for us an indication of what God would want to see coming to birth in our world."[30]

The big question is whether this can still happen, because the relationship between symbol and reality, as we said, has become problematic for moderns. For modern people, as a rule, things are no more than their function of usefulness and certainly bear no reference to the Creator. We have acquired the habit of viewing things from the perspective of scientific verifiability. The things that cannot be established scientifically — and they are many — do not really exist (in accordance with the rule that what my nets cannot catch isn't fish). As a result things lose their symbolic, referential meaning and are reduced to their usefulness. As carriers of many meanings concrete things are reduced to univocal signs — formal objects as science handles them, things as pure functionality. The situation illustrates the degree to which the scientific approach has penetrated our daily lives. A telling example is water, which is characterized generally by

29. For a somewhat more elaborate description, cf. H. R. Blankesteijn, "Een begin van beweging," in *Mededelingen van de Prof. dr. G. van der Leeuwstichting,* no. 56.
30. R. Boon, "Liturgie vieren: is dat nog mogelijk?" *Eredienst* 2 (1968): 2-4.

its physical-chemical structure (H_2O). But at best that is a half truth, for concrete water, as we saw in chapter 1, has much greater meaning.

C. Verhoeven has strikingly characterized the resulting situation as one "around the emptiness."[31] For the person to whom God is real, the symbol, he says, is the religious name of a thing — a name pointing only to God. The symbol is the revelation of infinity, an indication that things are not self-sufficient but derive their meaning from that to which they refer. However, the question of the meaning of things is now seldom raised because meaning as such falls outside the sphere in which scientific questions are formulated. This may sound rather theoretical, but we are nonetheless dealing with one of the most essential conditions of faith and spirituality.

A person who loses the symbol in the biblical sense will in the end become estranged from the Christian faith and its celebrations. It is the loss of symbol that constitutes the heart of secularization, because this loss makes religious experience an impossibility.

Not that symbols and dealing with symbols have altogether disappeared. For artists, especially painters, filmmakers, and poets, symbols are still vital and real, though this is an admittedly small circle of people. Still, the shifts that have occurred in art are very important in this connection. In painting, for instance, the fact that the ideal of faithfully reproducing nature has been abandoned and the search for, and effort to imagine, the deeper realities have replaced it — this points to a renewed sense of the multivalence of things. Something like this can also be observed in poetry,[32] where a shift has taken place from "the poetry of thought," following a certain train of ideas, as was in vogue until World War II, to a poetry that is evocative, filled with images, preconceptual. The image is no longer a metaphor or comparison but a symbol. Modern poetry

31. C. Verhoeven, *Rondom de leegte* (Utrecht: Ambo, 1969), pp. 155ff.
32. Ad den Besten, "Mythe als werkelijkheid van de hedendaagse poëzie," in *Dichten als Daad* (Baarn: Bosch en Keuning, 1973).

does not contain comparisons but is itself parabolic. One cannot
come to an "understanding" of this poetry by a careful analysis
of its concepts. One must "intuit the sense," make out its meaning as one undergoes the impact of the symbolism.

"But this intuitive understanding, this experience on the
basis of suspected meaning, is a more intense and more deeply
emotional act of knowing than conceptual understanding."
Thus Coen Poort depicts a new beginning in his poem "A Place
of Detention":

> I am writing you a sign of life
> patient one,
> not, mind you, of a big life
> that I have chosen for myself
> to inhabit as a city on a mountain,
> but of a beginning of life
> a birth
> in a place of detention.[33]

The ability to handle images and symbols, of course, presupposes the faculty of imagination. How does the imagination
work? By picturing reality, the resulting picture showing what
reality means to us.

Blankesteijn has said a number of good things about the
formation of images.[34] An image, he says, is a summary, an
arrangement that enables a person to grasp a piece of reality.
The formation of images leads to knowledge and control. One
makes images of things that are important and that involve
risks. This is the reason why in archaic cultures religion and
art are dominated by the image of fertility.

Hence, an image nearly always has elements of a counterimage. True, it is an ideal arrangement of the world, but it
also gives form to what we miss or to what threatens to elude

33. Quoted by Ad den Besten and partly taken over here.
34. H. R. Blankestiijn, "De oude god en de knappe jonge dokter,"
in *Mededelingen van de Prof. dr. G. van der Leeuwstichting*, no. 47, pp. 3402-
3408.

us, like fertility. Thus the image as counterimage is the portrayal of a lack. What are the ingredients that compose the images? That will depend on what we experience as our greatest lack.

The resulting images need not be composed of some or other material substance. They can consist of descriptions or word paintings, like the vision of the New Jerusalem in the Apocalypse. The material for the counterimages comes to us from the world of experience. Blankesteijn illustrates this point as follows: "For the politically conscious proletarian the ingredients of the counterimage are: the destruction of capitalism and its power structures, a society in which there is no room for solidarity with one's 'associates in distress.' 'And he took her in his strong arms' is something that does not fit in such a society. And when, years after the revolution, that scene is still an impossible or forbidden thing, you get ridiculous situations where two lovers stand facing each other under a brilliant moon to discuss the new five-year plan." (Let the reader ask herself just what churchly variant of this scene would fit here.)

The imagination that produces such images and counterimages, though it uses the material of daily experience, is also nourished by deeper motives of religion and worldview, which give it color and direction. For the Christian this means being nourished by the broad themes of Scripture. This fact also serves to underscore the importance of a good liturgy in which the biblical images that are able to illuminate our existence and be exemplary can function. But we are not dealing here with matters that are directly or easily available. The biblically inspired counterimages are visions rather than ready-made blueprints that could be realized in the here and now. We will never build the new Jerusalem. Nevertheless, the vision of it is indispensable because its themes embody the dynamics of redemptive history and give direction and perspective to our lives. The church of Christ lives by expectation, the vision of the Promised Land of which we read in Joshua, itself a prophetic book.

What we encounter here is that participation in a biblical vision is not only an expression, but also a source, of faith. In other words, believing leads to action, but action also influences believing. Celebration precedes reflection. This is true from the perspective of the history of religion as well as from that of developmental psychology. Ritual is an expression of believing, while participation in ritual helps in the development of one's faith and gives form to it (cf. the influence of feasting and fasting). The celebration of a liturgy, which includes ritual, is the beginning and the end of religion. P. W. Pruyser believes that the changed convictions of the Reformers were largely the result of reflection on the rituals involved in the administration of the sacraments in the medieval church. He also thinks that increasing secularization in Western Europe today is largely a form of unbelief in the traditional rites.[35] He believes that corresponding unbelief in the cognitive content of religious conviction is secondary. At the same time, says Pruyser, one witnesses attempts at ritual expression that tie in with the changed convictions concerning life, as, for example, in political protest marked by processions, banners, slogans, and songs. Hence belief and ritual go hand in hand. Where people neglect the ritual, the convictions that go with them tend sooner or later to be affected as well.

The ritual, the structures of celebration, proves to be more tenacious. It is a noteworthy fact that even where people become estranged from the faith, they nevertheless continue to cling to the rituals of baptism and burial. Similarly, one sees Jews continue their participation in the festivals even when they become estranged from the tradition of faith. But in liturgically underdeveloped faith communities, when people lose their grip on the cognitive content of the faith, the break is much quicker and more decisive.

Between the ritual and the creed stands the story uniting the two, the story that exists in virtue of the imagination. "In contrast to conceptual thought, which creates order by grouping things and ideas on the basis of similarity and dissimilarity and by abstracting concrete details and phenomena, the story

35. P. W. Pruyser, *Tussen geloof en ongeloof* (Baarn: Ambo, 1974), chap. 8.

creates order by allowing an event or intrigue to unfold in a certain time span and by depicting the events which were brought about by the historical actors."[36]

A story cannot function without imagination and fantasy. Both give expression to human creativity. In this regard human beings are created after the image of the creative God. Fantasy, what Harvey Cox calls "advanced imagining," is the condition for the focus on, and openness toward, a new future, one that is suggested in the stories of the Bible.[37] In the Western world fantasy has been greatly undervalued, notably by Sigmund Freud, but in the last few decades a fresh wind is blowing. Fantasy no longer means the end of rational thought; people are now inclined to view imagination and fantasy as functions of consciousness equal in value to other cognitive functions. The imagination molds experience with an eye to new forms as they arise, for example, in fantasy. Fantasy is more, however, than a mental function, something evident in ritual, which is also called "embodied fantasy." One can of course degrade ritual to a harsh and rigid set of regulations, but it is not that by nature. We should rather speak of a formal structure in which freedom and fantasy can "twist and tumble." On this point Harvey Cox's remarks about ritual are illuminating. "It provides the person with a series of movements in which he is given access to an enormous wealth of human feelings. But these feelings now become the material for his own escapades in creativity."[38] Form and structure, freedom and creativity, presuppose each other. Also, formlessness and absence of fantasy usually go together.

Imagination and fantasy also play an important role in tradition.[39] Of that which comes down to us in tradition — the life story of man and his interaction with God — we form a

36. Ibid., p. 219.
37. Harvey Cox, *The Feast of Fools* (Cambridge, Mass.: Harvard University Press, 1969), chap. 4.
38. Ibid., p. 75.
39. R. Boon, "Aspect van dubbelzinnigheid in de Verlichting," in *In de Waagschaal* 11, 20 (1983): 10-17.

picture for ourselves. This picture, the result of imagination in which are also incorporated the experiences and feelings it elicits, enables us personally to assimilate the content of the tradition. This does not mean that we can fantasize with total abandon. On the one hand, the process of handing down the story is colored by the time in which the telling takes place; on the other, the tradition is marked by continuity. Tradition, one must remember, presupposes "a community of memory" in which the story is handed down from generation to generation. Even more important than personal assimilation is the fact that by one's imagination a person can enter into relationship with persons who come up in the tradition. In a common process of imagining these persons become recognizable figures. This communication is of great importance for the spiritual growth of man. Images become examples and inspire people to embody them in their own lives.

To say "fantasy" is to say "play." This is also true for liturgy. Guardini spoke of liturgy as play. In worship there is imagination, dance, and song; here a person may simply be a child of God, playing before his face. To play before the face of God is the essence of liturgy. "Liturgical education therefore also consists in this, that the soul learns not to look for a purpose in every action, not to want to be too goal-oriented, too intelligent, and too mature, but aims simply to live."[40] "Becoming as a child" applies certainly, if anywhere, to the celebration of the liturgy.

5. Intellect and Feeling

Pleas that more attention be paid to the shape of the liturgy often include the argument that in worship feeling is as much entitled to its rightful place as intellect. And who would wish to deny such a reasonable wish? At this point feeling is often

---

40. R. Guardini, "Liturgie als spel," in *Bron van leved water* (Den Haag: Lannoo, 1962).

viewed in relation to the aesthetic experience. The latter must not, then, be restricted to the experience of beauty. The tragic, the comic, the ugly, all constitute ingredients of the aesthetic experience.

Western civilization can be characterized as a "culture of the intellect" that reached a point of culmination particularly in the period of the Enlightenment. At the same time there was manifest a strong tendency toward privatization that also came to expression in the countermovements of Pietism and Romanticism and sometimes deepened there into individualism. In these movements feeling resumed an important role in reaction to rationalism, particularly as the link between religion and art.[41] The plea for restoring feeling to a position of honor, as it is being made again in our day, as a rule addresses itself to the expression of emotions. That, to be sure, is a good cause, but there is much more at stake.

In our discussion of "image" and "symbol" it already came up that reality can be approached in different ways. In general, three approaches can be distinguished.[42] In the first place, there is the intellectual, analytical approach. In this approach people assemble objective data by analyzing and explaining them. A plant, for example, can be analyzed in terms of all its parts, colors, and shapes. This is the scientific approach that attempts to establish the factual data.

In the second place, there is the approach that focuses on the utilitarian value of things. A section of woodland, for instance, is considered from the viewpoint of what it could be used for and what it would yield (in wood production, recreation, development potential, etc.). Central here is a thing's usefulness or utility. This approach, often in combination with the first, has come to dominate Western societies.

The third approach is directed toward the significance of things, their meaning and origin, toward their being an expres-

41. G. J. Hoenderdaal, *Het esthetische — een weg tot geloof?* (Baarn: Ten Have, 1982), chap. 1.
42. A. Verheul, *Inleiding tot de liturgie* (Roermond: Romen, 1964), chap. 5.

sion of and a reference to another, invisible, reality. Central here is the symbolic nature of things. This presupposes awareness of a spiritual world that is not directly observable, one that is known not so much with the intellect as with the heart. For the believer all that is created speaks of God. The poet Guido Gezelle put it this way: "When the soul listens, the universe speaks; it speaks in a language that is alive." The same awareness is voiced in the Psalms: "The heavens are telling the glory of God; and the firmament proclaims his handiwork" (19:1).

The apostle Paul has the same thing in mind when he says: "His invisible nature, namely, his eternal power and deity, has been clearly perceived in the things that have been made" (Rom. 1:20). Following in this tradition medieval man could speak of creation as "the footprints of God." Reality is the bearer of a secret that can be disclosed and known by way of the heart.

Moderns have become estranged from this third approach. As a result of the atrophied capacity to "read" images people have become largely unable to "see" the createdness of the world and the consequent symbolic character of reality.[43] Images, considered as bounded forms that sum up a complex world, do not touch the intellect as a conceptualizing tool so much as the deeper layers of the human minds, viewed now as the seat of the higher affections.

Feelings also constitute a way of knowing and relating to the world. It is precisely this aspect of the emotional life that has been so badly neglected in modern Western culture. As a rule, feelings are viewed as purely subjective, as no more than internal affairs that result from external stimuli — a sort of secretion resulting from observation and memory. But feelings are not, as sometimes claimed, a commentary inside one's consciousness on events taking place outside it. Feelings rather are a form of participation in the qualities of the world, a mode of responding to the values of the world.

After all, the world is multivalent, useful, enjoyable, deso-

43. H. M. M. Fortmann, "De religieuze waarneming in het oeuvre van Guardini," in *Alz ziende de Onzienlijke*, vol. 1 (Hilversum: Gooi en Sticht, 1974).

late, relative, and so on.[44] One could add many more words to this list, but the totality of it is concentrated in the faith experience that the world as creation points to the Creator. To deny ontological status and value to these qualities is more a matter of prejudice than of objectivity. It is through our feelings that we relate to the qualities of the world, and as such they are to be viewed as a way of knowing that world. Our openness to the world in which the observation occurs is of an affective nature, based on a relationship to the reality of love. It is an old bit of wisdom first voiced by Augustine and later reformulated by Pascal that one can only truly know a thing by loving it.

Furthermore, one author (Fortmann) was able to speak of feelings as "modes of communication," modes of relating to the world. In other words, we are talking about experiencing that which proceeds from other people such as seduction, threats, mollification, awesomeness, etc. At stake here are the qualities of things, emotional meanings that can only exist in communication with the world. Feelings are comparable, says Fortmann, to a bridge resting on two pillars, one situated in the experiencing person and the other in the world, the things to which we address ourselves.

Since the Renaissance people have increasingly denied the objective value of the feelings, broken down the pillar in reality, so that the bridge was suspended in midair. More and more things were attributed to human subjectivity. They became neutral, devoid of content, and observation consequently became impoverished. The world is no longer something that provokes human feeling. In consequence, primary contact with the world was lost, affective participation as a way of knowing disappeared, and feelings became denatured. Feelings lost their significance because "the meaning which things were supposed to give them was declared invalid, void."

Gradually the question, What do I feel? came to denote immersion in one's own feelings. Originally the intent of that

44. P. A. van Gennip, *Het kwetsbare midden* (Bilthoven: Ambo, 1973), p. 108.

question had been, What does this world mean to me? By their nature, feelings point to the outside world. If one now focuses attention on the feelings themselves, one separates them from the world to which they are directed. Systematic isolation of one's feelings in time destroys one's bond with the outside world. By this route people also lost the feeling (the awareness) that things point to God. It is no wonder — feelings had been degraded to pure subjectivity. That which was originally understood as referential was now declared to be mere fancy and projection. This is what the world was told from the seventeenth century on, and Freud restated it.

The result has been the impoverishment of human perception and observation and therefore also of religious perception. How did this happen? The fundamental idea at work here is that what is found in the world apart from the apparatus of science, and what therefore cannot be verified by scientific means, proceeds from the human observer and therefore has no objective value. This idea arose as a result of the overestimation of the Renaissance scientific method. Increasingly, scientific knowability became the criterion for the objectivity and reality of things. In virtue of its own character, science had to reduce the multivalence of things to one meaning, limiting itself to a single aspect. As a rule, these are the aspects accessible to sense perception, the numerical, the spatial, and the physical aspects. In the scientific analysis of things their symbolic value gets lost by definition. There can, in this context, be no question of the referential meaning of the creation. The expression "being created" loses its meaning. The idea that science is not competent to make pronouncements about the totality of things is a notion that, aside from incidental protests, was not to come up till the present century.

This rising intellectualism was carried through also in the view of man held in those days. Man, according to a much-used definition, is to be regarded as "an animal endowed with reason." Rationality and free will were for centuries the cornerstones of the established view of man. "Passive" feelings, characterized as irrational, came to stand over against the "active" intellect. Feelings were no longer viewed as typically human but were said to belong to the lower things that humans and animals have in common. The result was that in the end there was little or no room in psychology for the higher or more spiritual feelings, the affections.

In reflecting on this material one needs to realize that feelings are not simply natural endowments, any more than observation is. Both of them develop only in the course of a long process of learning. One can say that the vital feelings (sensations) associated with the organic functioning of humans (hunger, thirst, satiation, and the like) are in principle natural endowments, though these feelings, too, need to be more precisely developed and incorporated into a more comprehensive framework of experience. However, higher or spiritual feelings such as love, hope, joy, happiness, and a sense of beauty have to be developed and are therefore highly dependent on the culture in which a person grows up. It is here that contemporary Western culture shows a serious deficit. Think, for instance, of the underdevelopment of the emotional aspects of eroticism and sexuality.

All of this raises the question concerning the role of rationality. The fact that theoretical thought, particularly scientific thought, has come to control our daily experience, and has become for us a kind of second nature, is sad; but it is no reason to start doubting rationality as such. Rational thought is a great blessing. The idea, however, that rational thought is self-sufficient or the highest authority in human life has proven false. Problems result not so much from the nature of rational thought as such as from its dissociation from the total context of human existence, the context in which it originally had its place. After the Renaissance culminated in the Enlightenment, a split occurred between rational thought on the one hand, and feeling, imagination, and intuition on the other. Modes of knowing other than those of abstract theoretical thought were rejected, such as the thought that operates through concrete imagery and is associated with feeling, imagination, and intuition. In the course of time people began to accept abstract thought as "normal," while they viewed concrete thought as passé — still present only in children, artists, and nonscientific cultures. This process of intellectualization, in which conscious thought became ever more important, has also had its influence on the life of faith. A clear example of this involves the arguments on the basis of which the participation of children in the Lord's Supper was (and is) opposed. In a rationalistic manner, knowledge and consciousness were (and are) advanced as precluding such participation without regard for the life of believers in the biblical world. It is a strange fact that in the discussion concerning the proper forms of association with God people speak in terms of knowledge and understanding while Scripture in many ways makes clear that humans are to relate to God primarily in terms of praise, of blessing the Name, of lament, and if need be of imprecation.

One often hears it said, by way of counterargument, that the issue, after all, is the Word. The Word is at stake, certainly, but it is the Word that has not yet been reduced to the categories of Western thought.

In Greek "word" has to be translated both as *mythos* and as *logos*. *Mythos* is the word as used in the sphere of intuition, and as it relates to imagination and feelings; it concerns the disclosure of a mystery and eludes the usual dimensions of space and time. *Logos,* on the other hand, is the speech of factual observation that occurs in the sphere of the intellect. Mythos and logos are corresponding notions that participate in each other, presuppose each other, and, when all is well, do not form a contrast.[45]

In mythos humans respond to experience with the faculty of imagination that presupposes thought. Logos lives by the same experience, but now the faculty of imagination recedes and the conceptual takes precedence. Mythos and logos are both the results of thought processes. In mythos the world is

45. This material was taken from J. Blauw, "Mythos-logos," in *Geloven en denken,* ed. A. Th. Brüggeman-Kruijff (Amsterdam: V. U. Boekhandel, 1982).

more than an object; it is a mystery. However, it is a mystery that can be reached neither by the imaginative power of the mythical mind nor by the objectivizing drive of logical thought.

In the liturgy, although the logos is not absent, mythos dominates: the word as sacred story that invites the worshipper to join the play and to celebrate. That is the undertone. Logos is the word that calls the worshipper to action and constitutes the overtone that vibrates to the undertone. Mythos and logos, in their distinctiveness, resemble feeling and intellect but actually reach farther, both of them having reference to the mystery of the existence celebrated in the liturgy.

In preceding centuries reason and imagination, intellect and feeling, have been made into opposites. Fact and fiction, present in every story and inseparable from each other, were opposed to each other as truth and lie. This rationalistic prejudice from the Enlightenment has to a great degree obscured our grasp of the biblical story. The result is an expression like "it says what it says" or "the Bible from cover to cover."

It is time that this fundamentalistic trend in our thinking, this product of conformity to the world, be unmasked as the cuckoo's young of the Enlightenment.

4. A Way to Go

Having taken note of all that has been said in the previous chapters and the problems cited there, one could reasonably ask whether liturgy can actually be done. Sometimes one hears the remark that moderns no longer know what to do with the biblical viewpoints.[1] The reasoning is quite simple: Everything that clashes with the modern mind has to go. People forget all too easily that our humanity is not simply a given. Being human is a trust and a mandate. In the Bible, becoming human is the central issue.

"Hence there is a difference between the language of 'Canaan' — the land of the future — and ordinary, everyday language. We come together as people who are in process, in search of our own 'shape,' and who are never done with that process; but we do get handed to us the provisional forms of which we believe that they are not too incongruous with what we shall be."[2]

Involvement with the Bible, a condition for this process of becoming human, takes shape in the liturgy. A biblically inspired liturgical celebration is not an anachronism but rather a critical

1. S. Krikke, *Veranderd levensbesef en liturgie* (Assen: Van Gorcum, 1976).
2. J. Verheul, "Liturgie in een geseculariseerde wereld," III, *In de Waagschaal* 7, 16 (1978): 12-15.

center of reference in relation to the shrunken structure of experience that characterizes moderns. This function of the liturgy presupposes a use of the Bible (we talked of this earlier) in which its stories are not approached from a modern historicizing frame of mind but rather understood from within their own context. Among other things this means that the ancient stories have the function of parables in which believers recognize the meaning of their own existence and the church gets an understanding of its own calling. It is a view of the Bible that regards it not as a collection of bits of historical information but as a future perspective in which "something more than the ordinary" becomes visible. As members of a community of believers you learn to relate to the Bible as a book structured in the main as "a book for public reading through all the seasons" (Barnard).

"And when this is how you relate to the Bible, you learn patience, you learn to sing doxologies, you unlearn the habit of clinging tightly to your definitions, of quitting too soon, of adopting the premature dictum. . . . You learn to live with an unfinished symphony."[3] And we do all this not under the influence of the motto "What does the Bible say about . . . ?" but simply by letting the Bible have its way with us. In the process we have to unlearn certain mistaken mental habits. By an abstract analytic approach to Scripture we miss the biblical mark. The goal is not to discover a system of doctrine or thought; it is to recognize and acknowledge the profound inner connection that holds the Bible together.

It follows from this that congregational singing is fundamentally important. In song what comes to expression simply cannot be stated in intellectual terms; the inexpressible is given voice. The singing person is one in whom heart, soul, and mind constitute a unity. When a person is in this condition words penetrate deeply into his or her inner self. "Every time a person sings this word anew, he appropriates it the more."[4]

3. W. Barnard, *Op een stoel staan*, pt. 1 (Haarlem: Holland, 1978), p. 55.
4. F. Mehrtens, *Kerk en Muziek* (Den Haag: Boekencentrum, 1960), p. 31.

Song also has an element of proclamation because it permits others to·share in that which is expressed. At the same time song is an expression of the unity of the church. Song can bridge gaps between people at points where discussion has ceased.

The hymn is not the only form of song. Music has a broader function because it breathes meaning into texts. Think of singing or chanting the texts of the Psalms in their unversified form. In this process musical accents direct the interpretation while antiphones convey the color or theme of the psalm. The form of a hymn is but one of several possibilities.

"The Bible played and sung in all available keys — that is the art which is called 'liturgy'" (Oosterhuis). The word as sung is the heart of the liturgy because it is always more than teaching; it is broader and deeper. "To sing is to fit yourself into a larger whole, to join your voice with that of many others; it is to take on words which you cannot live up to all by yourself, which you dare tackle only in conjunction with others."

"Speech, lecture, catechetical instruction alone cannot, as effectively and persuasively as a singing liturgy, interpret the many-sided significance of these (biblical) images: the experience of faith and human existence packed into them. It is the liturgy, consisting of songs and stories, which conveys to us the hope that all of this is true after all."[5]

It is well at this point to make emphatic reference to the place of children in worship. A primary condition in all liturgy would be that children from the age of seven or eight (when they can begin to sing along) can follow it. This does not mean that they should be able to understand it all. Who among the adults does? But there must be enough in every segment for everyone to follow the process. In this context the sung parts of the liturgy are indispensable. Music, movement, visualization, structuring the framework of experience — all help to prepare the field in which the Word is sown.

In this chapter I shall discuss certain proposals, offer some

5. H. Oosterhuis, "De tent der samenkomst," in *In het voorbijgaan* (Bilthoven: Ambo, 1975).

ideas of how liturgy could be done, how, in other words, we can relate to the biblical notions. It is not my intention to enter a discussion concerning the "ordinary," the fixed parts of the liturgy. For that purpose a number of introductions are already available.[6] I shall, however, offer a brief overview of the possibilities of the "proper," the changing parts of the liturgy from Sunday to Sunday. Preceding this there will be a discussion of the Easter Vigil, followed by a suggestion for the celebration of the Feast of Tabernacles as the second liturgical focus (in addition to Easter). The chapter closes with some remarks about the relationship between doing and hearing, liturgy and ethics, the celebrating church and a suffering world.

1. The Celebration of Easter as the Center of the Church Year

From the short account of the historical development of the liturgy in chapter 2 (sec. 4) we already discovered that from the very beginning Easter has been the center of the Christian liturgy. In the classical tradition — still an extremely meaningful framework for liturgical formation — preparation for Easter begins on the ninth, the eighth, and the seventh Sundays before Easter — the pre-Lenten period. These Lord's Days bear the names Septuagesima, Sexagesima, and Quinquagesima. After this introduction to Lent follows the period of forty days that includes the six Sundays of the period of preparation ending with Holy Thursday. On the evening of Holy Thursday (the new day beginning after sundown) Easter

6. Horton Davies, *Christian Worship: Its History and Meaning* (Nashville: Abingdon Press, 1957); H. Grady Hardin, Joseph D. Quillian, and James F. White, *The Celebration of the Gospel: A Study in Christian Worship* (Nashville: Abingdon, 1964); James F. White, *The Worldliness of Worship* (New York: Oxford University Press, 1967); idem, *Protestant Worship: Traditions in Transition* (Louisville, KY: Westminster/John Knox Press, 1989); Ralph P. Martin, *The Worship of God* (Grand Rapids: Eerdmans, 1982); Frank C. Senn, *Christian Worship and Its Cultural Setting* (Philadelphia: Fortress Press, 1983).

begins; it is continued on Good Friday as the Easter of the Cross and is concluded with the celebration of the Easter Vigil. After that, beginning on Easter Sunday morning, comes the joyful period of Easter, the fifty-day period extending till Pentecost.

In the following section we shall concentrate on the celebration of the Easter Vigil. The liturgical order described here developed over a period of decades and provides a possibility to involve oneself with the features of the classical liturgy.[7] The entire sequence consists of the Blessing of the Light, the Reading of the Scripture, the Baptismal Commemoration, and the Communion.

The Celebration of the Easter Vigil

The worshippers are received in a dimly-lit room decorated with many flowers. A brief statement of welcome indicates the theme of the celebration: "In it we remember and celebrate how God makes a new beginning with this world in the death and resurrection of Jesus Christ."

The Blessing of the Light begins with a short prayer and the singing of the Easter psalm, Psalm 118. Then follow the words:

Jesus Christ yesterday and today,
beginning and end, Alpha and Omega.
To him belong the times and the ages,
To him be all glory now and forever. Amen.

The Easter candle is lit as a symbol of Christ while the cantor and the congregation sing responsively:

Light of Christ — Lord, we thank You.

7. a. W. Barnard, *Binnen de tijd* (Hilversum: Paul Brand, 1964), pp. 107-18; b. "De Adem van het jaar," *Prof. dr. G. van der Leeuwstichting*, pp. 111-23; c. *Anders dan alle andere nachten*, Convent van Kerken, Hilversum, the Netherlands.

Cantor, choir, and congregation now sing a song in praise of Jesus Christ. What follows is part of a text composed by Huub Oosterhuis and set to music by Bernard Huybers; it is reproduced here as an example of an open, non-strophic form.[8]

Cantor: For you, people who are here present,
who know of death and darkness,
for You this prayer of praise
that is lifted up as a shining light.
Of Jesus Christ I sing to you.
He is the Word that was passed down to us
and that we pass on in this world;
we pray that the faithfulness of our God
may find a ready hearing,
that his new covenant may never die out.

Cantor: O holy God most high, we praise You,
puny as we are, with this voice
that you have created in us.
And on behalf of this world, all your people,
of that entire mass of people whom no one
   can count,
we adore and worship the glory and power
which you have disclosed to us in Jesus Christ.

Cantor: Be merciful to us, You who are mercy;
cause your mercy to shine upon us.

Choir: Be merciful to us, You who are mercy;
we trust You, Lord our God;
would you ever put that trust to shame?

Congregation: And would you ever put that trust to shame?

At this point the antiphonal song for the Lucernarium in the Easter Vigil, also by Oosterhuis and Huybers, can be inserted.

8. *De Paasnachtwake,* Werkgroep voor Volkstaalliturgie te Amsterdam (Hilversum: Gooi en Sticht, 1968).

Its refrain is: "Awake, O sleeper, and arise from the dead, and Christ shall give you light" (Eph. 5:14).

The Reading Service starts with a responsive prayer for the Easter Vigil:

Cantor: All people living wait for you,
Open your hand and we shall be satisfied.
Do not turn from us lest we die.
Do not let us fall back into the dust.

All: Send forth your Spirit and we shall be re-created.

Cantor: Flame of our life, light of our light.

All: Send forth your Spirit and we shall be renewed.

Cantor: Soul of our heart and light of our light.

All: Send forth your Spirit and we shall be re-created.

Cantor: Renew the face of the earth.

All: Amen.

A child now asks a question: "How is this night different from all other nights?" The father or mother offers the answer in which there are hints of the Scripture reading to come.

Cantor: This is the night of remembrance
in which heaven and earth are created
and people are called from darkness into light.
This is the night in which God led the fathers,
    sons of Israel, out of Egypt.
This is the night in which Noah and his family
    were saved.
This is the night in which Isaac allowed himself
    to be bound like a lamb to the altar and
    God himself provided a sacrifice.
This is the night in which God's Messiah broke
    the bonds of death and ascended from the grave.
This is the night of which it is written:

141

> If I say: "Darkness will cover me, then the night
> is a light all around me."[9]

From ancient times, during the night of Passover, there were readings from the Torah, from Genesis, and from Exodus, readings concerning creation, the flood, the sacrifice of Isaac, and the Exodus. Easter is the fulfilment of Genesis and Exodus (Barnard); to create is to redeem; on the third day God created the dry land, a habitable world withdrawn from the powers of evil and chaos. Light was created on the first day, the day that became the day of the resurrection.

These readings are taken from the synagogue liturgy for Pesach. They constitute a comprehensive Easter story celebrating victory over death. All creatures (Gen. 1), the nations (Gen. 5ff.), and the elect (Gen. 22) are involved. Apart from these four are eight more readings, especially from the prophets. As a rule one has to make a choice, but in any case there are good reasons for including the first four. The theme of every reading is announced as follows (each with a distinct voice):

"This is the night in which the world was called to life." Genesis 1:2-3 is read, each part interrupted by the singing of, "And there was evening and there was morning, one day, (a second day, a third day, etc)." Instead of a seventh day, "this day" is substituted.[10] After the reading, Psalm 8 is sung responsively: "O Lord, our Lord, how majestic is thy name in all the earth!"[11] (For that matter, tradition supplies a prayer with every reading.)[12]

"This is the night of salvation, of which the fathers have sung" (reading of Gen. 5:28-29 and 6:5-8). The sequel to this reading takes place in the form of a song:

9. *Anders dan alle andere nachten.*
10. Scheppingsverhall, in Oosterhuis/Huybers, *De nacht voor Pasen* (Hilversum: Gooi en Sticht, 1970).
11. *Liturgische gezangen voor de viering van de eucharistie,* No. 99 (Hilversum: Gooi en Sticht, 1975).
12. "De Adem van het jaar."

God saw that the sin of man on earth was great, yes, that there was no one who still honored his covenant and acted as was proper, no one except Noah.

Refrain:
How long, O Lord, can You tolerate the earth
  and the evil it does?
Will the flood destroy both the good and the evil?
Indeed not: You have mercy on Noah and his family.

God spoke: I have decided upon the end of the world. It is time to build an ark, Noah, for all living things; it is time to embark, Noah.

And when all was ready, according to God's command, Noah took his wife, his children, and some of all domestic animals, wild beasts, and birds, and placed them in the ark, as God had commanded.

Refrain.

When the waters rose, God the Lord remembered Noah and the ark. And God made a wind to blow over the earth; the waters subsided. The ark came to rest on dry land. A dove brought the news.

Refrain.

And as a sign God gave his bow to Noah: "In you I have established a covenant with every living creature I have saved alive."[13]

"This is the night in which God himself provides a sacrifice."
Reading from Genesis 22:7-14.
A moment of silent meditation.
"This is the hour in which the prophecies are fulfilled."
Reading from Isaiah 4:1-6.

13. From *Liederen uit de ark*, a stencilled collection of songs.

143

Following this, the canticle of Isaiah 5:1-7 can be sung.

"This is the night in which our fathers, the sons of Israel, were led from Egypt and walked through the waters on dry land."

Reading from Exodus 14:24–15:1.

The singing of a canticle inspired by Exodus 15, the song of Moses, is a possibility. Perhaps a spiritual like "Go down Moses" would fit.

This reading (and thus the entire sequence of Old Testament readings) is now concluded with the appropriate traditional prayer. A litany that petitions God to grant his grace and to redeem us from all evil is sung as a transition to the baptismal memorial. It is concluded with an extended "hallelujah."

The baptismal memorial itself begins with an exhortation: "Therefore, then, all you who have come to celebrate his faithfulness and confess the Name of God, to renew the covenant he has made with us and to confirm the election in which you are included together with the Messiah, raise your voice with might in order to make known the manifold wisdom of God; raise your voice and sing with me: "Let that mind be in you which was also in Christ Jesus, the Messiah" (the canticle of Phil. 2:6-11 follows).

Then comes the renewal of the baptismal promise and the memorial is concluded with a baptismal song:

Arising from the water
He leaves behind his old domain.
Henceforth both land and water
Are not the same again.

Then follow the words:

We kindle the light and share it,
We pass it to each other,
And we confess that Jesus Christ is the Light
of the world.

The deacons light their candles by the Easter candle, after which each person lights his or her candle by that of the other person's, so that the light "grows." Meanwhile the choir sings:

> O Light that rouses us each day,
> How cold we are beneath your early ray,
> We stand alone and unprotected.
> Cover me lightly, enflame me, [lead me to Light.][14]

When the light has been passed to everyone, the regular lights are switched on and the gospel of the Resurrection is read.

A deacon cries out, "The Lord is risen," others follow by shouting, "He is truly risen," and then all say: "The Lord is truly risen!" While singing "Rise Up! — An Undreamed-of Morning Dawns," worshippers leave their places and form a circle around the table.

Then begins the final part of the Vigil, the celebration of table fellowship. This may be either the Eucharist or a love feast (Agape). If the Eucharist is chosen, it is important to follow, also musically, a truly festive order of service made for the occasion. If the love feast is chosen, the members themselves ought to bake the bread, bread that stands as a symbol of daily life and can therefore serve as a symbol of self-surrender.

The participants stand around the table (for the reading of the gospel the candles have been lit) and first pray the words of intercession. Then follows the table prayer. In the event a love feast has been chosen, the table prayer could be taken from the Didache and concluded with the Lord's Prayer. The meal that follows is closed with a prayer of thanks for the Easter night and a song stressing that "the future of our Lord is here."

We repeat: the preceding outline is merely suggestive. Much depends on local possibilities. Having a love feast (Agape) imparts to the celebration a familial character that bears a lingering resemblance to the Jewish Seder. The Agape meal can also make a strong contribution to the "messianic"

14. *Liturgische gezangen*, no. 247.

atmosphere that ought to prevail at the celebration of the Eucharist but often does not.

It is to be recommended, not to say imperative, that the celebration of the Easter Vigil be preceded by preparation in the form of liturgical catechesis. In the absence of such catechesis much of the symbolism and typological coherence of the Vigil will be lost. The same is true for the celebration of the Feast of Tabernacles.

2. The Feast of Tabernacles as a Halfway Point

In the first chapter (sec. 7) we discussed the biblical backgrounds of the Feast of Tabernacles and in chapter two (sec. 4) we called attention to the fact that in the classic liturgy for the Ember Days in September there are echoes of the Feast of Tabernacles.

A celebration in the spirit of this feast would not be out of place in the church, considering the biblical mandate to celebrate this feast and the motives involved in it. Easter is the beginning, in a sense, and at the time of the Feast of Tabernacles another half year has elapsed: we are halfway between the Exodus and the Promised Land, in the middle of the wilderness. For the early Christians Israel's pilgrimage through the wilderness was a type of the church's journey as the people of God. "An ever returning theme in the catechesis of the early church was the wilderness journey of Israel. Camping in tents was a parable of the journey that led from slavery under the dominion of pagan powers, by way of the catechumenate (the instruction of candidates for baptism) and baptism, to the fellowship of the believers with Christ in the celebration of the Eucharist and to the liberty of the children of God."[15]

It is a harvest festival. The harvest is the biblical image of human destiny. Our lives have to bear fruit. It is also a messianic

15. R. Boon, *Op zoek naar de identiteit van de kerk* (Nijkerk: Callenbach, 1970), p. 191.

festival. Living in and journeying through the wilderness, we celebrate this feast as an oasis that both reminds us of, and leads us to anticipate, the Promised Land. It awakens hope for the coming of the Messiah and his kingdom. With reference to this perspective Barnard remarks: "Behind this world of created things, when mankind's long trek is over, there is the city which will descend from heaven."[16] "Behold, the dwelling of God is with men. He will dwell with them, and they shall be his people" (Rev. 21:3).

It hardly needs saying that a Christian celebration in the spirit of the Feast of Tabernacles must not be a copy of the Jewish festival. Such imitation would hardly be a sign of respect. However, the biblical motives of the Feast of Tabernacles, like those of the Passover, remain valid also for Christians. A Christian celebration, with a New Testament perspective woven into it, may be considered legitimate. One possibility is to embody these motives, by way of Bible readings, songs, and prayers, in a Sunday morning service. A good time for it might be the eighteenth Sunday after Pentecost, in the early fall. The psalm for this Sunday is Psalm 122, a pilgrim song. The Scripture reading could be taken from Deuteronomy 8, where the meaning of this feast comes through. Luke 13:6-9 relates the parable of the barren fig tree as a picture of God's patience toward our frequent failure to bear fruit. Perhaps a celebration on the preceding Saturday would be even better. Such a celebration could be situated around a meal as symbol of God's goodness manifest in another harvest. In the biblical tradition the common meal is a central feature in every celebration; a meal builds community.

In a large room decorated with tree branches, fruit, and flowers, gathered in a circle around the table, the congregation could proceed as follows.

After a few words of introduction in which the biblical motives for the celebration are touched upon, the service could start with the responsive singing of "Hear, O Israel" by Wim

16. Cf. W. Barnard, *Binnen de tijd*, p. 242.

147

Pendrecht.[17] In this song the theme of this festival as described in Deuteronomy 16:13-15 is brought to expression.

1. When the sun ripens the fruit on the vine
   And people glean the ears behind the mowers,
   Together thus the plowers and the mowers,
   And everyone who turns the grapes into wine.

2. Come to the feast and sing with one accord.
   A tabernacle shall give you ample space
   In which to give him the glory of your praise.
   For he who gives you joy is God the Lord.

5. Praise him with heart and soul, both here and there.
   Oh Israel, listen to your Father's voice!
   His kingdom is approaching, come and rejoice.
   Praise God the Lord always and everywhere.

Every verse is followed by a refrain.

After a prayer for the feast comes a song composed by Hanna Lam:

Just to go with a stick in your hand,
And not to know what you will eat.
Just to go with a stick in your hand,
Endlessly far is the Promised Land. . . .

During this song, the participants, led by the children carrying their musical instruments, march around the table singing and symbolizing the journey through the wilderness and the world on the way to the Promised Land represented by the fruit.

Then follows the reading of Leviticus 23:39-43 concerning the institution of the feast and the manner in which it should be observed. There is a children's song by Clara Asscher-Pinkhof that has the *sukka* or booth for its theme:[18]

17. Published in *Zoet hout goedkoper* 3, 1 (September 1980).
18. Published in *Zoet hout goedkoper* 2, 1 (September 1979).

2. The Feast of Tabernacles as a Halfway Point

Four little walls and a thatched roof,
Is it enough, is it enough?
So quickly then our dwelling stood:

Some reeds, some nails, some wood.
Hastily shaped into something steady
And look: There stands the sukkoh ready!

Psalm 118, sung and recited, follows. This Easter psalm
also figures largely at the Feast of Tabernacles. The first five
verses can be said responsively.

Voice:	Give thanks to the Lord, for he is good;
All:	His steadfast love endures forever!
Voice:	Let Israel say:
All:	His steadfast love endures forever!

The antiphon follows: "Look, this is the day the Lord has
made, come and rejoice in it." The psalm, either sung or chanted,
is continued. It is concluded by the sung antiphon.

Then comes the reading from Ecclesiastes (9:7-10), which
has been read at this festival from ancient times. "Let your
garments be always white; let not oil be lacking on your head"
(v. 8). It reminds one of the newly baptized in the Easter Vigil
who celebrated the Eucharist in white clothes. The theme of
Ecclesiastes comes through in a "Song of Life" by Oosterhuis.[19]

1. One generation goes and the next one comes,
      only the earth remains.
   The sun comes up, and the sun goes down,
   And breathlessly it starts over again.

5. Let him then take joy all of his days
   That are given to him under the sun,

19. *Liturgische gezangen*, no. 156.

149

Eating and playing and making of friends,
Doing all his hands may find to do.

Like the booth of the Feast of Tabernacles, the book of Ecclesiastes instills a sense of the provisionality of things. After the harvest we might be tempted to think we are secure. (However, living in a booth can also be regarded as a sign of solidarity with the many who have no roof over their heads, an appeal to be mindful of strangers and oppressed people, "for you shall remember that I brought you up out of the land of affliction.")

For the New Testament readings one may read selections from "the gospel of the Feast of Tabernacles" (John 7–9, e.g., 7:1-10, 37-40; 8:12).

Immediately following these readings comes a song about Jesus and the Feast of Tabernacles.

This song opens with a refrain:

The Lord — blessed be his name — speaks to us in Jesus' words.

1. Not yet has the time been born,
   The time which is in my Father's hand.
   The world by evil dreams is torn —
   A sukka wobbles in the sand.
   Refrain.

4. He who is thirsty must come to me and drink,
   for living water quenches the desperate desire,
   The spirit will make all people think —
   A sukka wobbles in the mire.
   Refrain.

The readings are concluded with Revelation 7:9-17. "After this I looked, and behold, a great multitude which no man could number, from every nation, from all tribes and peoples and tongues, standing before the throne and before the Lamb, clothed in white robes, with palm branches in their hands . . ." (v. 9).

On their way to the common meal as image of a common messianic future, the participants march in procession around the table while singing the song, "We've Heard It Said."[20] Its refrain goes like this:

> We're going, hand in hand,
> To the other side, the Promised Land,
> A land for our possessing,
> A land where God our glorious God
> Shall raise his hand in blessing.

The table prayer that is used is derived from the liturgy of the Easter Vigil (see chap. 4, sec. 1).

"Blessed is he who comes in the name of the Lord; Jesus, Messiah, come and deliver us, O son of David."

For the meal that now follows, the celebrants have baked the bread themselves. Because it is a harvest festival, the meal has a festive character; there is wine for the adults, grape juice for the children, fruit salads, and the like.

After the meal, a song is sung and a prayer of thanksgiving follows, beginning like this:

> We thank you and remember your deeds at harvest time, and receive the habitability of this earth as a gift from your Fatherly hand.

A pleasant way to end the celebration is to sing a round. An example is "Living Everywhere" by Oosterhuis.[21] Verse 3 reads:

> My home is nearly everywhere,
> This earth my heaven, my Father's there;
> The smile of the moon, the light of the star,
> People dreaming, yet know where they are. . . .

Zechariah 14:16-19, which underlies Revelation 7:9-17, makes clear the great importance of the Feast of Booths as a focal point for the nations.

20. Text by Wim Pendrecht, published by Benny Vreden Producties, Hilversum.
21. *Liturgische gezangen*, no. 194.

One might consider the idea of concluding the feast on the following Sunday — in line with the Jewish tradition — with a celebration in which the motifs of the Rejoicing in the Law (Simchat Torah) are central. In view of the fundamental significance Jesus attributes to the Torah (not an iota or dot will pass from the Torah until all is accomplished) such a celebration would not be out of place in the Christian church. As we noted earlier, on that day (the Simchat Torah) the conclusion of Deuteronomy is read as well as the first verses of Genesis, which speak of the formation of the dry land. This "dry land" which God separates from the primeval waters, a habitable earth wrested from the powers of chaos, is also an image of the Promised Land toward which pilgrims are moving under God's protection — as one realizes during the Feast of Tabernacles.

3. From Sunday to Sunday

In the church's movement from Sunday to Sunday the feasts continue to dominate, giving color both to the preceding and succeeding Sundays. The feasts, one must remember, are not so much incidental events as decisive moments in a continuum of the church calendar. In the Church Year, as that took shape in the West, the Christmas cycle and the Easter cycle are clearly structured by the feast in question. The feast of Jesus' birth is preceded by the period of Advent and followed by the time of Epiphany. Following this period comes the Easter cycle with a preparatory period called Lent and a subsequent Easter season lasting till Pentecost.

The summer time — the period of the "green" Sundays — does not have any such structure. In the background of the Sundays in the autumn, as we noted earlier, certain echoes of Jewish fall festivals are discernible, of which the Feast of Tabernacles is one. It remains a strange thing that the church has largely ignored the biblical themes that play a role in the Jewish fall festivals.

This is true, first of all, of the Day of Atonement. The idea that this feast lost its meaning as a result of the disappearance of the temple cult is a little too simple. Postbiblical Judaism can make clear to us that more is involved here than the retention of a historic relic. In principle the same applies to the celebration of New Year, or Rosh Hashanah, a day of self-scrutiny and penitence when people concentrate on God's majesty and judgment.

The period in which these feasts occur, the time of the "Days of Awe," calls for penetrating liturgical analysis and reflection in the church. W. Barnard has made a start in this. The point of this involvement should be not to attempt to annex the Jewish legacy or to engage in a form of philosemitic imperialism, but to listen patiently to the biblical notions and to allow oneself to be instructed in this regard by Israel, the people of the Messiah. In view of Jesus' own attitude and conduct, one can hardly conceive of any other approach. Torah and Gospel are very closely related.

Barnard makes this clear, for instance, by relating the nineteenth Sunday after Pentecost to the Simchat Torah that takes place in the synagogue about that time. Matthew's Gospel (22:1-14) speaks of the horror of missing out on the wedding feast and landing in "the outer darkness." According to Barnard, one must listen to such a parable against the background of the Torah readings on Simchat Torah, specifically the beginning of Genesis: "And God said: let there be light." Continuing, he writes: "Of course, the people who believed that in Jesus' Easter sacrifice they had found the messianic wedding heard such a connection between the words that made the rounds among them and the Torah with which they had been familiar from their youth. For them there was no alternative but to understand the language of the Messiah in the context of the Torah! This is precisely the source of their *simchah* (delight)! With this understanding they were convinced they had chosen the right way (Ps. 119:1). They were the ones who belonged to the Way (Acts 9:2). And that way was the true exodus."

The foundational feasts have been taken up into the church calendar. The Church Year is a mirror of world time as subject to the claims both of God's redemptive action and of individual human existence. However, although different Lord's Days are "colored" by the feasts on the church calendar, the question remains how from Sunday to Sunday we shall deal with the Scriptures, particularly with the Old Testament. We have already ascertained in chapter 1 (sec. 2) that the ancient notion, already popular in the days of the church fathers — that the Old Testament is obsolete — is untenable. One might summarize the insights regained as follows.

We shall have to train ourselves to read the Scriptures "from the perspective of the gospel, using the Old Testament as starting point." The reason is that the New Testament itself regards the gospel as the perspective in which the Old Testament comes into its own. This idea, as R. Boon has demonstrated,[22] is the result of the following considerations:

1. As is evident from the interpretation of the Scriptures by Jesus and the apostles, the New Testament presents itself as an explanation of the Old.

2. The language of the New Testament, "the total complex of the basic words of the Bible together with their meanings and linkages," is rooted in the Old Testament.

3. In view of the numerous quotations and allusions present in the New Testament, the Old Testament is clearly presupposed.

All this constitutes an argument for a continuous reading, Sunday after Sunday, from the Old Testament in combination with a reading from the New. The question is how to give practical form to all this: the handling of the foundational feasts and the continuous reading from the Old Testament. To all this there is also a pedagogical side. A congregation not at all used to working with an established lectionary would do well first

22. R. Boon, "Enige opmerkingen naar aanleiding van de Schrift als traditie," *Eredienst* 13 (1979): 7-20.

to acquaint itself with the larger structures of the feast cycles centered in Christmas and Easter. There is excellent material available to us for this learning process.[23] Here we find the basic information concerning the Church Year, particularly as it took shape in the Western church. Here, too, we find the readings from the Old Testament, the Epistles, and the Gospels that go with each Sunday.

By working with this information we discover all kinds of typological connections between the Old and the New Testament. However, in this plan there is some arbitrariness in the selections from the Old Testament; they rather constitute an anthology, and remain stuck in the schematism of prediction and fulfilment as regards the coming of the Messiah. Readings from the Torah are rare. Hence a number of efforts have been undertaken to do justice to the Old Testament without losing the fundamental lines of the Church Year.

A first possibility has been developed — better, tracked down — by W. Barnard.[24] He distinguishes several story cycles. The first ten chapters of Genesis constitute prehistory. The first cycle runs from the patriarchs to the entry into Canaan, with Moses as the central figure (Torah). The second cycle, preceded by Judges again as prehistory, runs from David to the captivity, along with Elijah as the central figure. A third cycle concerns the captivity, along with the books that relate to this period. In this arrangement Barnard sees a parallel with the division of the generations in Matthew. From Abraham to David, from David to the captivity, and from the captivity to the coming of the Messiah, are periods of fourteen generations each. This entire complex then culminates in the story of the Transfiguration on the mount: Jesus with Moses and Elijah. "The Law and the Prophets *happen* in the Gospels," says Barnard.

He proposes a double sequence. At Easter the story of

---

23. *Proclamation: Aids for Interpreting the Lessons of the Church Year*, 24 vols. (Philadelphia: Fortress Press, 1973-75).
24. Cf. W. Barnard, *Binnen de tijd.*

Adam is read; the remaining stories of primeval history (Gen. 1–11) follow in the Easter season. At Pentecost the first cycle begins with the calling of Abraham. In the fall the stories of Jacob and Joseph follow. At Advent the Exodus stories begin (Moses as mediator), followed by "the travel journal" of Numbers and "the syllabus of Deuteronomy." The entry into the Promised Land falls in the Lenten period.

In the second cycle the prophetic books are read, preceded by Judges as a second prehistory ("the middle ages of Israel") in the Easter season. The book of Ruth, the ancestress of David, is read at Pentecost. The stories concerning David are read in the summer, those concerning his sons in the fall, and those about Solomon in the Christmas season. Elijah is featured in the period before Easter.

The parallels between these two cycles, as well as those between these cycles and the readings from the gospel in the Church Year, are striking.

A second possibility is suggested by one liturgical team.[25] Their point of departure is the assumption that in Jesus' days the Torah was read through over a period of three years. This method was said to correspond with the fact that in the Torah each of the Jewish feasts occurs three times. These feasts were used as "hinges." For example, Passover occurs in Exodus 12, Numbers 9, and Genesis 4. Since Passover corresponds with Good Friday, we have in hand the guidelines for a continuous reading of the Torah over a period of three years. In this project the five books of the Torah correspond with the five successive books of Psalms. An attempt was made to combine the readings from Moses with the classic readings from the Gospels. This worked fine as far as the Christmas and Easter cycles were concerned. But in the summer season it did not. The readings from the Gospels are the ones that tend to draw listeners up close. It is a fascinating attempt in keeping with the thrust of Jesus' words: "You search the Scriptures . . . it is they that bear

25. "Aan de hand van Moses," pts. 1 and 2, *Mededelingen van de Prof. dr. G. van der Leeuwstichting.*

witness to me" (John 5:39). A striking illustration is the reading on Good Friday of the story of Cain and Abel from Genesis 4. The reading from the Epistles in this scheme is sometimes done during the celebration of the Eucharist.

Although this summary is far from complete, it does offer an impression of how the Old and the New Testaments can jointly function in the liturgy. In passing we must say a word about the participation of the children. In most places there is too little concern for them, while in reality what is involved is the future of the church. A real possibility, in whatever church-school setting is available, is to work with the children for several weeks on projects leading to specific services that the children have a real share in staging. This can take a number of forms — the singing of an appropriate or specially composed song, a play or group dance depicting the Bible story, or the making of collages. In some cases the children can be involved in the public reading of Scripture and in the intercessions.

4. Hearing by Doing

From time to time the question comes up whether we can celebrate at all — break the bread and share it — as long as we acquire our daily bread at the expense of others. However, neither a positive nor a negative answer to this problem resolves the tension.

Certainly celebration must not be allowed to live a life of its own, detached from solidarity with suffering fellow human beings. In Christ we are united with all the people of this world and, knowing this, we can speak about liturgy as "listening to the heartbeat of the entire world."[26] It is, of course, not true that relationship to God can be reduced to interhuman relationships and that liturgy is simply a derivative of these relation-

26. T. J. van Bazel, "Luisteren naar de hartslag van de wereld," *Rand de tafel* 37 (1982): 136-41.

ships. Still, in the church's celebrations the awareness of a suffering creation may never be absent. "Prayer . . . without a social engagement degenerates into sentimentality, while social engagement without prayer turns into something grim or even barbarian."[27]

Christ is still in pain on account of this world. For his followers it cannot be otherwise. A restoration of the Kyrie Eleison to its original role in worship ("Lord, have mercy"), the prayer for a suffering creation in the form of a litany, would not be out of place in the church. Before the Gloria, and certainly before bringing up its own needs and sufferings, the church prays vicariously for the world.

In this respect, too, there is much to learn from the Jewish tradition. The Hebrew word for liturgy, *avoda*, also means "labor." The commandments have a bearing not only on one's daily conduct but also on the liturgy. Behind this truth is the idea that the whole of human existence is worship or "liturgy," including the responsibility for creation and particularly one's fellow man. Prayer for us is often an expression of a personal need, but in Judaism prayer is a command from God and involves praying the fixed prayers that developed over the centuries. The Jewish worshipper is thus spared the enormous burden of the modern person who believes he or she has to compose his or her own prayers, since originality is what counts. Unfortunately, as a rule our own "spontaneous" prayers tend to be a concatenation of cliches. The range of the fixed prayers that come down to us in tradition, both Jewish and Christian, is so much bigger. This also means that tradition offers us a broad scope for self-expression.

Adoration and praise presuppose order. Without some kind of rite the soul cannot lift itself to God (Levinas). The rule here is that by doing one comes to hearing and understanding. While action is part of the "liturgy of life," liturgy has an ethical aspect. Only that person succeeds in doing righteousness who

27. E. Schillebeeckx in an interview with Huub Oosterhuis, *Werkschrift voor leerhuis en liturgie* (1981): 25.

imposes a rule upon his or her own nature. The ritual directions of Judaism are subordinate to the cause of righteousness. This ritual, says Zuidema, is training in self-limitation, in respect for one's fellow man and for nature.[28] Anyone who violates creation violates the glory of God. In the Jewish liturgy one often encounters the thrice-holy invocation of Isaiah 6:3: "Holy, holy, holy is the LORD of hosts; the whole earth is full of his glory." In the liturgy of the Eucharist this passage occurs in the Sanctus. In his use of creation man must master himself, which is also the background of the Jewish purity laws. The precepts are not there for their own sake; they exist to remind people of their appointment as stewards of creation. Thus liturgy and ethics constitute a single whole. In that whole there is much for Christians to learn and to celebrate. When Moses read the laws of the covenant to the people, they answered, "All that the LORD has spoken we will do, and we will be obedient" (Ex. 24:7). This commitment was interpreted to mean: "In the doing we will hear."[29]

28. W. Zuidema, *God's Partner* (Baarn: Ten Have, 1977), chap. 9.
29. Ibid., pp. 176-77.